Progress and Perspectives

THE CATHOLIC QUEST FOR CHRISTIAN UNITY

by GREGORY BAUM, O.S.A.

SHEED AND WARD — NEW YORK

FOREWORD

EVERY TIME I have addressed audiences of priests and laymen in Toronto and other cities of Canada and the United States, I found that Catholics were extremely interested in the contemporary movement for Christian unity in the Church and other Christian communities. I have always found Catholics most eager to learn the new attitude which this movement has produced in the Catholic Church and quite ready to revise many of the inadequate ideas they had entertained about Protestants. Catholics instinctively understand that all Christians ought to be one, and they are quite willing to accept that, for the sake of this unity, they should do their utmost to remove obstacles and prepare the way.

My Protestant audiences also manifested great interest in the attitude of the Catholic Church, and many of the insights which have become the acquired possession of Catholic ecumenism for a generation seemed quite new to them and a happy surprise.

This general concern has prompted me to write these pages. The following chapters contain much of the material I have used in my talks and conferences. This book is not a work addressed to scholars. While writing it I constantly had in mind the lively and attentive faces looking at me from the audiences in the many halls where I had spoken. It is to people like them that I address myself in these pages.

In the following I take for granted the theological basis of the Catholic ecumenical movement. We believe that the Catholic Church is the one true Church of Jesus Christ, united to him as his earthly body; but we also believe that men outside the Church in good faith who confess Jesus Christ as God and Savior and are baptized in water and the Holy Ghost are truly Christian, reborn in Christ, alive in the Spirit, and hence, despite their separation, our Christian brethren. I take for granted in these pages that Christian faith and supernatural charity are found in communities beyond the visible boundaries of the Catholic Church, and that Christians guiltlessly separated from us have access to sacramental grace and spiritual life. A clear statement of these doctrines is comparatively new in Catholic theology. In my book *That They May Be One* I was able to show that they are in perfect harmony with papal teaching.

This book is not written simply to give information. It is also a plea. Its purpose is to create a sense of urgency among Catholics. There is so much we can do for Christian unity, even as lay people. We must find new dimensions of Christian charity; we must discover a new vision of the Church's ecumenical task; and we must pray and suffer for unity knowing that these are the mainsprings of any renewal in the Church.

ACKNOWLEDGMENTS

THE AUTHOR wishes to express his gratitude for the assistance rendered him in many ways by his colleagues at St. Michael's College, Toronto, Canada. He wishes to acknowledge his special debt to Rev. John Madden, C.S.B., for his generous help in preparing the manuscript. He also wishes to thank Msgr. John Oesterreicher for his kind permission to reprint material from Vol. IV of *The Bridge*.

CONTENTS

Progress and Perspectives

THE CATHOLIC QUEST FOR CHRISTIAN UNITY

1

THE UNITY OF THE CHURCH

THE MISSION OF THE CHURCH is to render perpetual the work of Christ's redemption. Jesus died and rose for us; Jesus gave us the gospel of truth; Jesus has power to transform the heart; Jesus gives us access to eternal life. This work of his divine redemption is perpetuated by the Church which he founded. In her, Jesus continues to act on men as the Savior of the world. Through her voice, he makes himself known; through her sacramental gestures, he transforms our sinful hearts; through her rule, he leads us on the steep road to holiness.

Saying that the Church continues the work of the Savior does not mean, of course, that the redemption of mankind, worked and consummated by him, is incomplete. Christ has done everything. Lifted up above the earth, on the cross and in his glory, he draws all things unto himself. He is the one mediator between God and men, the one area of contact between the God of mercy and sinful mankind. But in reconciling the world with his eternal Father, Jesus, the crucified and risen Lord, has chosen men to be his helpers. These men, called and redeemed by him, become organs of the very redemption which has given them life. The brothers he elects to have a share in his divine vitality become his instruments in choosing others. Redeemed and united to himself, the followers of Christ make up a holy community in which the saving acts of the Redeemer are rendered present to mankind. In his Church, Christ remains in history.

This is Catholic doctrine. The Church, looked upon with the eyes of faith, is not simply an organization, not simply a human community, not simply an institution with doctrines, rituals, and rules. To him who believes, the Church is the community of God's choice in which the redemptive acts of Christ are present to all men. This is the heart of the German theologian Moehler's famous definition of the Church, written down in the last century, which has initiated a veritable springtime in Catholic ecclesiology.

The mysterious presence of Christ in the Church is due to the power of the Holy Ghost. "It is good for you that I depart," the Lord told his disciples, "for if I do not go, the Advocate will not come to you. But if I go, I will send him to you" (John 16:7). If Christ had remained visibly in our midst, he could have associated with very few of us in an intimate fashion. Leaving the world, however, and sending us the Holy Ghost, he found a way in which he could be present to us and in us, invisibly—yet in reality and power. It is in the Spirit, therefore, that Christ is head of his Church and united to each one of us. It is again the great Moehler, mentioned above, who has brought to the foreground of Catholic consciousness the ancient doctrine that the Church is in and through the Spirit.

If we did not understand this notion of the Church with its proper qualifications, it would be a frightening doctrine indeed. To say that the Church is Christ acting in history could be understood as a justification and consecration of the entire life of the Catholic Church in the world of men, including the political role played by the Catholic hierarchy in the past and at present. We could create the impression that we are endorsing the sins and shortcomings of the Catholic community in this world, that we try to attach the aura of sacredness to purely temporal decisions, and that we seek to invest the good sense of our leaders with a theandric quality. Such a misunderstanding would be tragic. If we say that in the Church Christ is acting in history, we mean that through her his power to save and sanctify becomes available to men of all ages enlightened by her and in all places where she is established. At the same time, however, the Church remains the Church of sinners. This too is Catholic dogma. *"Mea culpa, mea culpa, mea maxima culpa"* is the confession which the Church puts on the lips of every one of her children in her official liturgy. The problem of sin in the holy community of the Lord will occupy us further on. At this point we simply warn our reader not to understand in an unspiritual way the ancient Christian doctrine that in the Church the saving acts of Christ are present to mankind.

It is of interest to us, and a source of joy, that within Protestant theology a contemporary movement of great vitality has discovered Christ's mysterious presence in the Church. Since so many of us tend to think of Protestantism as a school of religious individualism, it is worthwhile to emphasize the great discovery of the Protestant ecumenical movement, exerting an influence on every branch of theology, that Christ has identified himself with his people. Here is a powerful statement taken from the *Report* of the Faith and Order Conference held at Lund in 1952:

Christ is the head of the Church which is his body. Through his Spirit Jesus Christ himself is present in his Church. Christ lives in his Church, and the Church lives in Christ. Christ is never without the Church, and the Church is never without Christ. Both belong inseparably together. . . . What happened to Christ in his once-and-for-all death and resurrection on our behalf, happens also to his Church in its way as his body. . . . The Church is called to continue the mission of Jesus Christ to the world, so that the way of Christ is the way of his Church.

Many Catholic readers will be impressed, and somewhat confused, by the above quotation. This sounds Catholic, they will say. How can Protestants say these wonderful things about the

Church, and then stay aloof from her? To understand statements such as the above, we must remember that the ecumenical movement has led a vast number of Protestant Christians back to the foundations of our faith, to the Scriptures, and the understanding of these Scriptures in the primitive community. These Protestants are passing through a process of discovering certain biblical elements which had been neglected by them for many centuries, or which had never really been seen by them at all. When they speak of "the Church," they do not refer to the Roman Catholic Church or, to be sure, to their own religious communities. By "Church" they mean the people of God, the community of salvation, which is announced in the Scriptures, and to which the faith of the Christian community gives witness. To this Church they wish to belong; in this Church they desire to encounter the Lord of life.

Jesus has come into the world to heal the wounds of humanity. He is a Savior. The mercy he manifested when healing his compatriots from sickness of the body becomes more evident still in his power to heal the more radical illnesses of God's humanity. This indeed is the significance of Jesus' frequent miracles: they announce his power over the evil forces which corrupt and destroy the creation of God.

We are accustomed to saying that the Lord saves us from sin. If we cling to him by faith, he will liberate us from the slavery of sin. This doctrine may also be worded differently. Remembering that the fall of man brought us hate and destroyed charity of man to man, we may say that the wound in our midst which Jesus has come to heal is—our disunion. This will become clearer in the following paragraphs.

It is the teaching of the Scriptures—and in this its doctrine is unique—that mankind is one single family and that all divisions in this family are the fruit of sin, against the divine order, and the source of perpetual misery. This is one of the main points of the biblical account of creation: all men are the children of a single couple. All men, however widely they may differ in appearance or custom, are related to one another as members of the same family. It is not simply some definable human nature, philosophically conceived, which creates the bond between peoples. No, according to Genesis, all men are descendants of one and the same human couple. To emphasize this doctrine of unity even more, to show that there is no essential difference between man and woman, the account of Genesis still goes further. We learn from the inspired author that Eve the woman was taken from the very substance of Adam the man. This story announces in unmistakable terms that all human beings are derived from one single person created in the image and likeness of God.

The Bible rejects all theories current in pagan cultures that the human family is divided into castes and classes which are natural to it. The Bible rejects the views so widely spread among ancient civilizations that women are essentially inferior to men. No, according to the Word of God, man is one. In the eyes of the Bible and of the Church, all theories about the origin of men proposing several ancestors, or ancestral tribes, seem exceedingly dangerous. They could be made to serve as factors dividing the human race, as if we were no longer blood relations. For the Bible, the divisions of mankind into factions and parties are due to sin. After the first transgression the sons of Adam and Eve came into conflict: and murder, enmity, and divisions were the results of their encounters.

It is into this world of division and strife that Jesus brings the victorious power of his charity. Men are to be one again in love. Men are to forget and forgive all that divides them and love their neighbor as themselves. They are to be concerned about the other more than about themselves. They are to imitate the selfless service of the Master and help their fellow human being. While enmity and strife divide, the Christian following the Gospel is called to transcend the barriers of hate. We are to love our enemies. We are to love all men without exception.

The redemptive work of Jesus in favor of human unity, however, was not confined to presenting an ideal of sanctity. Not only what our Lord taught, but also and especially what he did, must be considered if we are to understand his unifying mission. He died and rose for all men tainted by the sin of Adam, and thus became the second Adam, father of a new generation, the first-born of many brothers who were to be united by the bonds of grace. Sharing the same new life, living from the same divine Spirit, all men are brought together into a community which is so intimate and spiritual that it is called a body, an organ, a unity of a new kind, an image of that supreme unity existing in the very Godhead between Father, Son, and Holy Spirit. "That they may be one" Jesus prayed, "one" as he and his Father.

Jesus, then, came into the world to heal our divisions, yet the unity he produced in our midst far exceeds the unity of the first creation. As the new Adam is superior to the first, so is the unity in Christ superior to man's unity in Adam.

Faithful to our ecclesiological principle that the Church continues the work of Christ in the world, we must say that the mission of the Church was, is, and ever remains the healing of the wounds of the human family. In particular, the Church is sent to form a new people, in which all men are to be transformed. The new creation the Lord has promised, which would remake the human household in holiness and light, is already taking its beginning in the Church's mission to heal the divisions of nature by the unity of grace.

If it is true that the great forces dividing our generation are the pride of race, the selfishness of class struggle, the accumulations of group egotism, ideals of conquest, and religious or antireligious intransigence, then we must claim that the Church was sent to heal all of these. In her are found the means to overcome and transcend these barriers. In her, Christ is at work unifying humanity.

This is a startling doctrine. If it is true, it should be a natural thing for Catholics to take a leading part in the universalist movements of our times. Meditating on the mystery of the Church, we should be more open than any other group to all that leads to the unification of mankind, the bridging of differences, and the overcoming of barriers. The history of our century, however, has not always borne out this supposition. It is true, we have the magnificent example of our recent Popes. But we cannot deny that in our Catholic communities there are as many isolationists as among non-Catholics, as many separatists, men with limited and parochial outlooks, men content with the barriers which sin has erected. Yes, so great is the evidence against the universalism of our Catholic witness that we may well ask the question whether this universalism is really firmly established in Holy Scripture. It is really true that from the beginning the Church was sent into the world to unify mankind, to bridge human differences by the charity of God, and to draw all men into the one body which is Christ's own here on earth?

One of the most startling revelations of the Church's mission to unite the human race was made on the first day of Pentecost when, according to the Book of the Acts, the Spirit descended upon the apostles, filled them with divine power, and made them speak in foreign tongues. At that time Jews from every nation under the sun were gathered in Jerusalem, and we are told that they were amazed and bewildered when they heard the apostles speaking each in their own languages. "We have heard them speaking in our own languages of the wonderful works of God," they exclaimed. What is the meaning of this miracle of tongues? Why do we call it a revelation of the Church's mission to unify mankind?

To understand the full significance of this miracle we must realize that it was the second miracle of tongues recorded in the Scriptures. The first one took place at the dawn of human history. It is contained in the story of the Tower of Babel. We are told that men on earth spoke one single language. Working together, they made preparations for the building of a city possessing a tower, the top of which was to reach the heavens. They wanted to be where God is; but God punished them. He confounded their language; no longer could the people converse with one another. They had to abandon the building of the city and were dispersed all over the world.

We have here a divine judgment on human pride. Man, trusting in his own powers, believed that he could lift himself up to the abode of God and make himself the master of life. He repeated the gesture of the first sin: seeking to be like unto God. But again he was punished. We are told, and this is profound biblical theology, that the punishment consisted in being divided into sections and groups without a common means of understanding. The Bible teaches us that the origin of the divisions of mankind into nations and classes is human pride. They are not the fruit of God's holy creation, but the result of human self-seeking.

We often read the opinion that the Old Testament does not know the doctrine of original sin. This is partially true. However, we do find a doctrine in the Old Testament which bears a certain resemblance to St. Paul's teaching of original sin. From the Bible we know that the Hebrews were hostile to human civilization and city life. The episode of the Tower of Babel is a clear example of this attitude. Among the prophets and holy men of Israel there was the suspicion that civilization and culture, that is, the works of men transcending the necessary requirements of life, were sources of moral corruption and seats of hostility to the divine. While Israel had an optimistic outlook on creation and human life as coming from God the creator, this outlook was profoundly qualified by their rejection of human culture as an expression of rebellious pride. The Hebrews believed that man was good, but their repudiation of the higher forms of culture meant that they suspected some seed of evil in man which gained in power whenever men labored together for goods beyond the necessities of life.

Against the background of the Tower of Babel and the sinfulness of human culture, the second miracle of the tongues on the day of Pentecost has a most significant message. At the Tower of Babel the tongues were divided and the unity of man was broken up; at the second miracle on Pentecost the divided people are able to hear again one single message, the barriers of many languages are removed, and the unity of man is restored. The Holy Ghost, coming to the apostles and confirming the Church in her mission, clearly announced that he would heal the wounds of the divided human race. On the first day of her existence the Church manifested, through the Spirit, that her mission was to unite all men into the community of Christ's love. The Church was sent to recreate one human family.

We may mention in passing that in this manifestation of the Spirit, reversing the division of tongues at Babel, we have the biblical root, at least one of them, for the positive outlook of the Christian Church on human culture and the progress of civilization. There is a possibility, with the Spirit as guide, of building a human society, a city, which is the expression, not of man's pride, but of his unity and mutual service.

There is another biblical theme expressing in a stronger way still the Church's mission to unify mankind. "In Christ," St. Paul announces to the Galatians, "there is neither Jew nor Greek" (Gal 3:28), and since, with this reconciliation, all the other divisions of mankind are healed, he continues, "there is neither slave nor freeman, neither male nor female. For you are all one in Christ Jesus" (3:28).

The schism of mankind into Jews and Gentiles may be said to be of divine origin. It was God who made a covenant with his chosen people, giving them the Law as a teacher of holiness and a protection against pagan influences. The Law was the unshakeable barrier between Israel and the nations. St. Paul, however, in the light of his own theology, looked more deeply into the origin of the Law and discovered that its promulgation by God was related to human sin. We are told that as a consequence of Adam's fall, mankind lived in darkness, idolatry, and human hate, and that the God of mercy, deciding to redeem the human family, gave the Law to Israel, the people of his own choosing, in order to reveal to this people the sin of the world which ignored its maker and the sins of their own hearts in constantly revolting against God's laws. The Law, in Paul's theology, brought sin to a head and prepared the conscience of mankind, of Jew and Gentile alike, for the merciful intervention of God in Christ's death and resurrection. The apostle writes: "The Law intervened that the offense might abound; but where the offense has abounded, grace has abounded even more" (Rom 5:20).

To understand the full meaning of the reconciliation between Jews and Gentiles, we must remember that the Law for Paul was a symbol bringing to light all the disorder in the world. Established by God, it became the exalted screen on which the malice of mankind revealed itself. The divisions among nations and tribes, the tensions between the sexes, the enmity between parties and groups, all these countless manifestations of human hate cutting asunder the human family, were summed up and symbolized in the opposition, produced by the Law, between Jew and Gentile. Being a divine gift, the Law was not sin; but it was meant to reveal sin. It made sin deliberate, spiritual, and supremely offensive to the divine Lord. Healing the deep division between the Jews and the nations, therefore, meant for Paul the removal of all other dividing forces from the human race. In all his letters, the unity between Jews and Gentiles in Christ immediately implies the reconciliation of all hostile groups and the disappearance of hate. Through the renewal in Christ, "there is no Gentile and Jew, no circumcised and uncircumcised, no Barbarian and Scythian, no slave and freeman" (Col 3:11).

To realize the full impact of Paul's doctrine, we must consider the tremendous emotional forces which accompanied Israel's separation from the Gentiles. A deep sense of fidelity to God's Law and all the conservative instincts of man to ancient traditions combined to erect a wall between the Jews and their neighbors which seems insurmountable. The Jews believed that the barrier had been erected by God to preserve the purity of their faith, and hence they were willing to suffer from the inconvenience and the odium of their voluntary segregation. Their contempt of the nations was not a racial, biological, or secular thing, such as we see today in certain areas between White people and Negroes living in their midst. With the ancient Jews the judgment on the nations was more deeply ingrained, making a separation more radical than any apartheid, but this attitude was of purely religious origin. A Gentile could become "a God-fearing one" (a friend of the Synagogue) or even a circumcised proselyte; he could enter the blessing of the Law and eventually have his children integrated into the people of Israel.

From the Acts of the Apostles we know how long it took the Jewish Church of Jerusalem to understand the radical universalism of the new faith. The message of the Lord, though addressed only to Jews, was so universally human in its appeal that it had meaning, immediately and without translation, for all men of whatever nation. But this universal aspect of the Lord's teaching was not strong enough to convince the primitive Church of the universality of salvation. They realized, of course, that the risen Lord was the Savior of mankind, but they were inclined to think that all men were to become Jews first and then, as members of the people of Israel, were to share in the blessings of their Messias. The reception into the Church of Cornelius, the centurion, uncircumcised and not subject to the Law, was a new and startling event which the Acts describe in great detail. We learn that God worked several miracles to convince the reluctant apostles to let Gentiles into the Church without first becoming Jewish. Peter needed a special vision before he understood that the universality of Christ's redemption did away with the barrier between Jews and Gentiles.

The Church of the Twelve in Jerusalem, even after it came to understand the catholicity of the gospel, preached the reconciliation between Jews and Gentiles with a certain reserve, careful not to offend Jewish sensitivity and minimize their own veneration of the Law. Paul, however, as we learn from the Acts and from his epistles, made the abrogation of the Law the very center of his preaching: "In Christ every one who believes is acquitted of all the things you could not be acquitted by the Law of Moses" (Acts 13:39). And what was the reaction of the Jews in the synagogue to Paul's sermons? They turned away from him, believing him to be an enemy of Israel.

Against this theological and emotional background, let us listen to the central passage in which Paul expresses the mystery of unity in the Church of Christ:

Bear in mind that you, the Gentiles . . . were at that time without Christ, excluded as aliens from the community of Israel and strangers to the promises of the covenants, having no hope [in a messias] nor [the true] God in the world. But now, in Jesus Christ, you [Gentiles] who were far off, have been brought near through [the shedding of] the blood of Christ. For he himself is our peace. He it is who has made both [peoples] one. He has broken down the enmity, this dividing wall, in his own flesh. The Law . . . he has made void, that of the two he might create in himself one new man, and make peace and reconcile both in one body to God by the cross, having slain the enmity in himself. And coming, he announced the good tidings of peace to you [Gentiles] who were afar off and to those who were near [the Jews]; because in him we both have access in one Spirit to the Father (Eph 2:11–18).

The significant point of this powerful passage—significant in our context—is that the unity between Jew and Gentile which is here proclaimed is a symbol and a guarantee of universal reconciliation. It is made quite clear that the peace between Jews and Gentiles is not the fruit of social agreement, or of political compromise. Rather is it the result of a more radical transformation of human nature. The image of God which man had lost, at least to some extent, is recreated in the man Jesus Christ; and through this elevation all differences due to sin, and due to the Law related to sin, are cancelled out. In Christ we are one: one people, one body. We have here the center of Paul's teaching on Christ's mystical body.

Paul explains in this passage that Christ, dying gloriously on the cross as the victim of human malice, has destroyed in himself, through his resurrection, the very malice which crucified him. Pride and hate have been slain in him, in his own flesh. The source of all divisions among men, the root of strifes and wars, resentments and competitions, have been removed by Christ. Even the greatest and most significant division in the world, that between Jews and Gentiles, has been healed in the Lord who has made one holy community in himself of the two separated peoples. Paul compares the wall of separation between Jews and Gentiles to the dividing wall in the Temple keeping the Gentiles away from the sacred precincts reserved for believing Jews. This wall has been pulled down in Christ, and with this wall fall all the other barriers which serve to divide humanity.

The communion which is promised us in Christ, however, does not fully belong to this world. It is to be visible in this world, as Christ himself was visible, but the intimate union to which we are called is one that reaches to the invisible realm of the divine. We are not only one people; we are one man in Christ. We are transformed individually by sharing in his nature; as a group we are transformed by constituting an organic unity of which he is the chief principle, the head. We live in him. We share in his joys, we have a part in his surrender to the Father. We are a priestly people. Paul announces that in Christ we have access to the eternal Father.

When the apostle calls Christ "our peace," he proposes a doctrine which is infinitely rich in meaning. Christ is our peace, first of all, because in him we find forgiveness of our personal sins. He is our peace because this sin, a source of social conflict and division, is removed by him; he is our peace because the most radical human schism between Jews and Gentiles is taken away, because the nations of the world enter into the community of Israel. He is our peace because he constitutes us as the family of one faith and charity; more than that, because he raises us as a community into vital union with himself. He is our peace, lastly, because in him we have access to the eternal Father: we become his children, sons of God. We too live in the bosom of the Father with the only-begotten One.

When Paul announces the reconciliation between Jews and Gentiles, it is this *peace* that he proclaims. And when we speak of the unity of the Church, then, we do not simply refer to the unity of Catholics visibly organized in this world; we really mean the peace of Christ creating unity in the human race. We believe that the Church has been entrusted with this peace of Christ, and hence by the unity of the Church we mean precisely the quality whereby the Church of Christ is able to heal all division in the world, and to integrate all men and all nations into the newness of life in the one man Jesus.

This brings us to a third theme of the New Testament announcing the unifying mission of the Church of Christ: the doctrine of universal reconciliation. Again it is Paul who is our teacher here. This time, he announces a unification in Christ which still goes beyond that symbolized by the union of Jews and Gentiles. Paul proclaims that through Christ God has reconciled unto himself all of humanity and the entire cosmos.

The central area of the divine work of reconciliation is sinful humanity. "When we were enemies, we were reconciled to God by the death of his Son" (Rom 5:10). Without any merit on our part, without any contribution made by us, Jesus Christ, triumphantly dying for us on the cross, destroyed the power of sin and cancelled the guilt oppressing the human race. The crucified and risen Lord restored us, at least radically, to the perfect image of the first creation and elevated us far beyond this into a new nearness and fellowship with God. Man in Christ is renewed, not according to the likeness of the first, but of the second Adam. If it is true that sin, the first sin of man, and all those that followed in its wake, have ravaged the face of humanity and distorted the harmony intended by God, it is also true that in Christ, God has re-established this first harmony by lifting up man to a true, though invisible, share in the glorious humanity of his eternal Son.

According to Paul, the Old Testament gives us ample evidence that with the fall of man, a general disorder entered the entire universe. The created universe was, in God's intention, so profoundly united that the conflict set up in humanity disturbed the whole order of nature. Nature became, to a degree, hostile to man. Birth shall be painful; weeds shall cover the fields; animals shall be dangerous to man. Sickness, corruption, and death, which is the way of all flesh in the present order, are due, in Pauline thought, to the first sin of Adam. The disorder in God's creation initiated by man is even reflected in the world of angels, though on this point the Scriptures do not tell us much.

Following the same principle, St. Paul announces that the reconciliation of man with God will be accompanied by the reconciliation of the entire universe. All the wounds inflicted upon the world through sin shall be removed. Human society shall be redeemed. Strifes, enmities, and divisions among peoples shall be overcome. "At one time," St. Paul writes, "you were estranged and enemies in mind through your evil works. But now he has reconciled you in his body of flesh through his death, to present you holy and undefiled and irreproachable before him" (Col 1:21). This reconciliation does not stop with man. Perfect unity shall return to the universe. According to the famous passage of Paul in the Epistle to the Romans, "Creation itself will also be delivered from its slavery to corruption into the freedom of the glory of the sons of God. For we know that all creation groans and travails in pain until now" (Rom 8:21, 22). The reconciliation wrought by Christ shall be universal. "It has pleased God the Father that in Christ all his fullness should dwell, and that through him he should reconcile to himself all things, whether of the earth or in the heavens, making peace through the blood of the cross" (Col 1:20).

This doctrine of reconciliation forbids an individualistic misunderstanding of Christianity. The view that the message of the gospel is salvation offered to the individual has little encouragement from the Bible. It is formally rejected in the great vision of St. Paul in which the justification and sanctification of the individual are linked to a wider transformation at work in the universe, uniting the human family into a community of love and reconciling all things to their Creator.

We learn moreover that, from the viewpoint of God, this reconciliation is complete in Christ. The great divine event in human history was the death and resurrection of the Lord. At that moment all things changed. In him the power of reconciliation became present for all times, in him the sin opposing it was broken down; in him all things are already re-established in harmony. In this sense, therefore, we may say that the Church is complete on the cross; in this sense we may say that the risen body of the Lord contains in embryo the entire new creation, the new heaven and the new earth. With Christ's victory a radical transformation has taken place in the universe.

Since the redemption of Christ does not produce grace in our hearts unless we believe in him and are baptized, we are sometimes tempted to limit Christ's transforming power to those who are personally united to him in charity. According to the theology we have just presented, however, the destiny of humanity and the situation of the world have changed with Christ's victory even prior to our acceptance of Christ's benefits in faith. Things are simply different now from what they were before his coming, quite apart from our reaction to him. If creation groaned before to be redeemed, and if society yearned before to be delivered from the yoke of injustice, this longing has now taken on a new, triumphant quality. For the reconciliation of the universe has been irrevocably established in Christ.

From this it follows, it seems to me, that the modern movements so clearly visible in human society toward unity, social equality, and common sharing, have a special religious significance. Unknown to themselves, and often in open conflict with the gospel, the men of these movements are really longing for and seeking that unity into which humanity has been lifted through its universal Redeemer. By the same token, the efforts of mankind to control the forces of nature, to heal diseases, extend human life and conquer the limitations of space, are expressions of creation's groaning made confident by Christ's victory. This quest may be purely secular in intention, yet the man of faith recognizes in it a manifestation, however limited, of the universal restoration of all things into the harmony of divine creation. Even the professedly irreligious man who yearns and labors for human community and the healing of nature's wounds is inspired, despite the error of his other convictions, by forces that proceed from the victory of Christ.

It is true, of course, that the reconciliation with God is a supernatural event, that it is wrought in an order superior to history; but in the economy of Incarnation, which is ours, there is no spiritual effect which does not make its imprint on the visible order. To believe that the reconciliation brought by Christ has no implication for the history of mankind and the lives of men on this earth, could only be inspired by a theology which does not take seriously the Incarnation of God in the man Jesus. It is not the first office of the Church to supply the inspiration which unites men politically and establishes a just social order, but the Church would not be the earthly body of the Lord if she failed to have this unifying and sanctifying influence on human society. As Pius XII said in *Negli Ultimi* (1946):

> The Church is firmly fixed at the centre of human history, as in a field moved and agitated by divergent forces, exposed to attacks which threaten her unity. Far from being shaken, however, she unceasingly radiates her own proper life of integrity and unity by sending new forces into a torn and divided humanity, forces meant to heal and to reconcile, unifying forces of divine grace, forces of the Spirit, Unifier of men.

In connection with his doctrine of universal reconciliation, the Apostle Paul clearly states that the Church's ministry is to extend this reconciliation to the world. He writes, "All things are from God, who has reconciled us to himself through Christ, and has given us the ministry of reconciliation. For God was truly in Christ, reconciling the world to himself by not reckoning against men their sins, and by entrusting to us the message of reconciliation" (2 Cor 5:18, 19). The first meaning of this office of reconciliation is, of course, the extension of Christ's forgiveness to those who will believe and be baptized. The mission of the apostles, and with them of the entire Church, is to free men of their sins and to sanctify them in the living body of the Lord. Since the ministry of the apostles is to apply the total reconciliation present in Christ, we assert that the Church is sent to heal the wounds of humanity, to overcome the barriers that divide men against men, and to restore the unity of the human family on this earth.

The Church's mission to unify mankind, therefore, is firmly established in the Scriptures. It belongs to the essential core of the good news. It is from this vantage point that we must understand the Church's gift of unity. As we have mentioned above, we must not regard this unity as a static quality of the Church's structure, but rather as a dynamic quality inclining the Church toward humanity and imbuing her with power to remove the obstacles that separate men.

The unity of the Church is a term frequently employed in Catholic literature. It is sometimes considered as a *note*. By this is meant the visible, external unity of the Church, that is, the historical links binding together Catholics in the unity of the same faith, the same rites, and the same government. Such considerations we find especially in treatises on apologetics. The emphasis is here on what can be proved to those who do not share our faith. Since we, the Catholics, have this note of unity, we may conclude that the promises of the gospel that the Church be one are fulfilled in our midst. This may well be a legitimate way of looking at Christ's gift of unity, but it neglects the whole area of deep meaning we have discussed above. Unity, in our context, is not a proof, but a message! Unity is possessed by the Church, but it qualifies the Church not only in regard to itself, but rather in regard to the world, to others, to humanity.

The unity of the Church may be considered more theologically as a *property*. By this we mean something much deeper than the visible, observable unity; we mean the totality of links by which Christians are united among themselves and with their risen Lord, of which—needless to say—the invisible ties are the strongest. The unity of the Church, as property, includes all the gifts of grace and charity which Christ has acquired for mankind on the cross. And yet, even here, we often have the tendency to understand this unity as a property relating members of the Church among themselves and to their head, instead of seeing, at the same time, the outgoing, dynamic, and missionary character of unity. According to the theology presented above, the unity of the Church inclines the Christian people to encounter the world and empowers the Church to heal the obstacles to unity set by sin. The unity of the Church is not closed, bending the Church back on itself, creating a new barrier in this world; on the contrary, it is open, making the Church a center from which unity proceeds, radiating into humanity the unifying power of divine grace. We may say then that the unity of the Church is not conservative, but missionary.

In the light of what we have said so far, it appears that the Church is in a real sense responsible for the world, especially for creating that unity in the world which is pleasing to God. In a more direct way—and this is important for our subject—the Church is responsible for the unity of Christians. While all Christians seek the unity Christ has promised, the Church does so with divine urgency, conscious that she bears in herself the power to overcome all obstacles to unity.

The Church's call to unify mankind in this world does not here concern us directly; but in the light of the biblical concept of unity, it is worth mentioning that the Catholic Community should be a vital source of those actions which favor social and political unity. Catholics, more than other men, should have a wide view of things, be deeply concerned about their fellow man, and have an international and social outlook in the political field. This corresponds to the mission of the Church. The papal encyclical *Mater et Magistra*, dealing with men's common good in this world, has set down once again that the Church's concern for social justice is not just a peripheral or accidental one, but part and parcel of her essential mission. To be Catholic means to feel responsible for all men.

This preoccupation with the unity of the human race is not always found in Catholic communities. Often, we seem to oppose the forces of history. Often, we have become so involved with a political or economic system that we feel bound to defend the *status quo* in order to protect our own survival. It has happened again and again in history, and we see signs of it in our own century, that revolutionary forces violently oppose the Church not because she proclaims universal redemption in Christ, but because she is thought to have become involved with political or economic powers preventing unity and social equality. In a deep sense, the

Church is always superior to, and radically independent from, any earthly power, and hence it is always unjust to oppose her for accidental ties with a particular social class. But this sovereignty of the Church is only recognizable to men of faith. In her members and her hierarchy, the Church may well be in solidarity with particular groups in opposition to the unifying forces in society, unifying forces of which she, in a deeper sense, is the very center. It is painful to see the Church persecuted because of her loyalty to Christ, but it is an infinitely more terrible anguish to see the Catholic Church opposed and suppressed for reasons other than her loyalty to Christ, that is, for reasons of her temporal alliances.

Since we are dealing here with the ecumenical spirit, it is the Church's responsibility for Christian unity that is of greater concern for us now. The Church, as we have seen above, has been endowed with the peace of Christ, she has received the power to advance our reconciliation in Christ, and hence she bears in herself the remedy for all the ills of our divided Christianity. By a curious paradox, the Church is more responsible for Christian unity than the communities which left her in the past. Responsibility in this regard is not determined by the degree of personal guilt or by other historical factors; rather, it is contained in the divine mission the Church has received from her Lord.

These biblical and theological considerations give rise to an attitude which is fairly new in the Catholic Church. Looking upon the divisions of Christendom, the Catholic Church, following her deepest inclination, will ask herself what she can do to become more Catholic, to remove all obstacles to unity, and to be renewed interiorly unto a more vital possession of Catholic truth. It is sometimes believed that the Catholic Church works for Christian unity by converting individual Christians to her creed; yet the proportions of our disunity are so enormous and have shaped so powerfully the history of centuries, that it would be unrealistic to consider the quest for individual conversions as a true confrontation with the burning problem of Christian disunity. This confrontation takes place only in the ecumenical movement. The theology of this chapter suggests that the Catholic ecumenical movement is not so much a way of influencing others, or of reminding others of what they should do, or of carrying on negotiations with them. Ecumenism is, rather, a movement within the Catholic Church herself, renewing her life and worship according to the pattern of Scripture and the liturgy, discovering the universality of her vocation, and making room in herself for all Christian values and authentic spiritualities, even those found imperfectly outside her borders.

Through the ecumenical movement the Catholic Church seeks to be transformed according to the image of perfect unity and catholicity, ineradicably imprinted on her substance by the Lord. The ecumenical movement brings to the surface the hidden wealth of the Church's unity.

2

THE EVOLUTION OF ECUMENISM
IN PAPAL PRONOUNCEMENTS

THE ECUMENICAL MOVEMENT within the Catholic Church is comparatively new; it has become respectable only in the last few years, especially in North America. The Catholic theologians concerned with Protestantism and with Protestants used to be looked upon with suspicion, and the suggestion that a Catholic theological renewal could flow from a dialogue with separated Christians would have been regarded as extravagant or disloyal. It is only since the convocation of the Second Vatican Council and the courageous speeches of Pope John XXIII that the ecumenical movement has been received with favor in the Catholic community of this continent. The last few years, therefore, have seen many changes in the relations between Catholics and Protestants in the United States and Canada.

In this connection we must recall the far-reaching significance of the establishing of the Secretariat for Promoting Christian Unity at Rome by John XXIII. For the first time in the history of the Church we now have an official ecclesiastical body through which the Church can enter into dialogue with Protestant Christians. This event has stimulated and encouraged dialogue with Protestants in all countries, even with groups which had hitherto shown some reluctance to do so.

At the same time, there are still many Catholic theologians, especially in North America, who are somewhat cool toward the ecumenical movement. They are made uncomfortable by it; to them it smacks of compromise. Many of them were used to an ardent apostolate for individual conversations, and they feel that to dialogue with others in friendship would be an act of disloyalty to truth, and a disservice to those in error. These opponents of the ecumenical movement can cite many papal and episcopal documents of the past which suggest that the only approved conversations with non-Catholics are arguments in favor of the Catholic faith. As late as 1928, Pius XI felt that he had to condemn the Protestant ecumenical movement because he believed it to be based on the erroneous presuppositions that all Churches are equal, and that Christian unity is to be achieved through compromise in matters of dogma. It is not surprising, then, that many Catholic theologians, trained only in these ways of the past, find great difficulty with modern ecumenism.

We cannot deny that Catholic thought has undergone a considerable development in regard to ecumenism. Development is part of Catholic life. The gospel was entrusted to the Church once and for all at the beginning of Christianity, but through the centuries questions arose in various parts of the world which could be answered only by meditating more carefully on the gospel, and by discovering the deep and often hidden implications of the Word of God. All was in the gospel at the beginning, but much of it was only implicit. In the course of the Church's history, the explicit content of the gospel unfolded in the mind of the Catholic community, as all Catholic theologians admit. Occasionally, however, Catholic writers who are quite convinced that there has been development in the past, reject the idea that we ourselves are passing through a stage of doctrinal development at this time. This is, however, exactly what is happening in our century. Our thought is undergoing a development, and one of its aspects is our relationship to Protestant Christians.

I am convinced that the evolution of ecumenism is part of a larger development taking place in the Church at the present time: our relationship to others, to outsiders, is undergoing a transformation, whether these outsiders be Protestants, Jews, members of other religions, or men with no religion at all. In our lifetime the attitude of the Church toward the human community has undergone a considerable change. Today the co-operation of Catholics, in the temporal order, with men of different religions has become a normal practice. We have become more conscious of our common humanity. Never before have we realized so deeply that the Church's attitude toward the world of men is a *signum Ecclesiae* (a note of the Church), a sign carefully watched by others, meant to reveal that her message is from Christ. Does the Church really love her neighbors? This is the question which Catholics, under the leadership of recent popes, have been asking themselves; and this is the question which thoughtful men outside the Church have been constantly putting to us. If we do not show forth this universal charity as the sign of our faith, our preaching will lack credibility.

In this chapter we wish to study this development with respect to dissident Christians. It would be interesting to trace this evolution in the great theological writers of our century. We shall confine our examination, however, to the papal documents themselves.

Let us consider, first, the Church's outlook on the separated Orthodox Churches. The beginning of a change in attitude toward these groups can be observed in the writing of Pope Leo XIII. This pontiff tried to create a new climate of friendship and respect for the dissident Churches of the East. In his encyclical *Praeclara Gratulationis,* he used expressions which had rarely been employed in Roman documents before.

We cast an affectionate look upon the east, from whence in the beginning came forth the salvation of the world. Yes, and the yearning desire of our heart bids us conceive and hope that the day is not far distant when the Eastern Churches, so illustrious in the ancient faith and glorious past, will return to the unity they have lost. We hope it all the more, since the distance separating us is not so great.

Leo XIII described the traditions of the Eastern Churches with appreciation and love, and when he called them to return to unity, he stressed that this call was not inspired by political or worldly motives. "The Church does not covet power, nor is she urged by selfish desires," the Pope wrote. His longing for unity was from the gospel.

In this encyclical, as well as in other official documents which followed, Leo XIII chooses his vocabulary very carefully. He does not wish to insult the Eastern Orthodox; he never calls them, or speaks of them, as schismatics. He seeks to describe the original rift in a way that would be faithful to his own convictions and yet would not be displeasing or insulting to the Christians of the East. He does not speak of schism. Instead, we hear: "As the ages rolled by, the waves of suspicion and hatred arose, and great and flourishing nations were dragged away, in an evil hour, from the bosom of the Roman Chuch." For Leo XIII the Orthodox are Christian brethren separated from the Church, or "dissident Christians." In the apostolic letter *Quam Nuper* he expresses "his good will toward clergy and people of the Eastern Churches, the united and the separated ones." All this is new in Roman documents!

Leo XIII reveals a deep appreciation of the Eastern traditions. He is conscious that their heritage is different from ours in regard to both the liturgies they received in antiquity and the mentality responsible for developing the ancient gifts. In the letters of the great Pope we find the recognition, still somewhat veiled, that Western Christians must make an effort of their own to understand their brethren of the East. The effort in the quest for unity, then, is not all on the side of the Eastern Christians; we too must exert ourselves.

This is the reason why Leo XIII took a great number of practical steps, accompanied by exhortations and encouragement, to build up faculties of Oriental theology among the Eastern Christians in union with the Holy See. In his encyclical *Christi Nomen* he writes that for the sake of the future reconciliation "we must multiply as much as possible the institutions where Catholic wisdom and practice are being taught, and taught in such a way that they are found in harmony with the genius of each nation." Leo XIII believed that the Catholics of Eastern rites should act as mediators between East and West, interpreting for us the ancient traditions of the East, and opening the Eastern mind to the universality of the Roman Church. In the apostolic letter *Orientalium Dignitas,* the Pope expresses his hope "that the Catholics of Eastern rites should live in such a way that they be regarded as true messengers and reconcilers of the holy unity between the Eastern Churches and the Church of Rome." Again, this is a new emphasis in Roman documents.

We find another theme in the writings of Leo XIII which touches a still deeper level of the mystery of the Church. While the Pope's letters are filled with longing and desire for unity, the image of this unity is always conceived in terms of differentiations. Though he stresses that unity is Christ's gift to the Catholic Church, he is equally aware that this unity becomes more luminous, more convincing and attractive, yes, more evangelical, if it embraces a great diversity of rites, customs, and forms of life. The gift of unity which Christ bequeathed to his Church is announced to the world, not through a rigid uniformity, but through a generous universality.

For this reason, Leo XIII looks on the Eastern liturgies with joy. In his letters, he emphatically declares that Oriental Christians need not fear that a reconciliation with the Roman Church would diminish the independence and authenticity of their own traditions. In *Praeclara Gratulationis* the Pope writes: "There is no reason for you to fear that we or any of our successors will ever diminish your rites, the privileges of your patriarchs, or the established liturgies of any one of your Churches." If, in the past, the Roman Church has sometimes created the impression that differences in rite or custom were only tolerated, Leo XIII insists that, far from being a concession on the part of the papacy, the diversity of rites is a glory and an ornament to the entire Church. Repeatedly he refers to that glorious queen of the Psalms (Ps. 44), who is clad in raiments threaded with gold, composed of various patterns in many colors: *Regina . . . in vestitu deaurato circumdata varietate.* May this be a symbol of the Church.

Beginning with Leo XIII, the Roman documents express a great respect for the ancient rites of Eastern Christians in union with the Holy See. The tendency to latinize is looked upon askance. In *Orientalium Dignitas,* Leo XIII explains the significance of the Eastern rites in the Church and introduces a number of canons to preserve these ancient customs against innovations from Latin sources. He justifies the new legislation: "The preservation of these Eastern rites is of the greatest importance. The splendid antiquity which makes these various liturgies so precious is an ornament for the entire Church and an affirmation of the divine unity of the Catholic faith." It is in diversity within community that the unity of Christ becomes manifest to the world.

The approach to Eastern Christians taken by Leo XIII has determined the policy of the papacy for more than a generation. In all the documents on the Eastern Churches since Pope Leo's time, we find a friendly, brotherly tone, a gentle call to reconciliation, and a recognition of the ancient traditions of the East. Every pope since Leo XIII has repeated the solemn promises, first made by him in *Praeclara Gratulationis,* that the Eastern Churches would not lose any of their liturgical and ecclesiastical traditions were they to return to unity with Rome.

With Pius XI the concern for Eastern Christians becomes even more intense. As we read his numerous statements on the question of unity and reconciliation, we discover a number of new elements indicating that the evolution continues. First, we detect a new humility. The Roman pontiff admits that the responsibility for the original separation is to be sought on both sides, and he asserts that the prejudice and ignorance which have perpetuated and aggravated the division existed, and still exist, on both sides. In *Rerum Orientalium* the Pope writes: "Many evils in the past and eventually the sad dissension itself . . . were the necessary result of mutual ignorance and national contempt. From prejudiced opinions followed a lasting estrangement of minds." The Pope admits our share of the guilt. For the first time, the official documents of the Catholic Church concede that the obstacles to reconciliation are not all on the side of the Orientals. Pius XI stresses that all of us have to change, all of us have much to learn, all of us have a long way to go before the union willed by Christ can come about. In the same document he states: "The remedy for the great ills of separation cannot be applied unless the impediment of mutual ignorance, contempt, and prejudice be first removed." In another letter (*Nostis Qua*) the Pope writes: "There is no hope of progress, unless the absurd opinions are dropped which in the course of centuries the ordinary people have acquired about the doctrines and institutions of the Eastern Churches."

With this new humility goes a deeper realization on the part of Pius XI that the separated Eastern Churches are alive with grace and holiness. Not only do his letters attribute to them the glories of ancient liturgies and rites, but they also express the confidence that these sacramental elements are filled with supernatural charity. The Pope writes of the Eastern Churches: "They have faithfully preserved the great part of divine revelation. Among them is found a sincere obedience to Christ, a special love of his holy Mother, and the frequent reception of the sacraments." In a longer passage, which has become famous, the Pope expresses his deep sympathy for the Oriental Churches, and he suggests that in the work of reunion new means must be found and applied: we must love one another, get to know one another, and free ourselves of preconceived ideas. This beautiful passage, written over thirty years ago, is well worth quoting in its entirety:

For a reunion it is above all necessary to know and to love one another. To know one another, because if the efforts of reunion have failed so many times, this is in large measure due to mutual ignorance. If there are prejudices on both sides, these prejudices must fall. Incredible are the errors and equivocations which persist and are handed down among the separated brethren against the Catholic Church; on the other hand, Catholics also have sometimes failed in justly evaluating the truth or, on account of insufficient knowledge, in showing a fraternal spirit. Do we know all that is valuable, good, and Christian in the fragments of ancient Catholic truth? Detached fragments of a gold-bearing rock also contain the precious ore. The ancient Churches of the East have retained so true a holiness that they deserve not only our respect but also our sympathy.

This leads us to a third new feature in Pius XI's attitude toward Eastern Christianity. The Pope insists in an altogether unprecedented way on the necessity of study and research. In the encyclical *Rerum Orientalium* he treats at length of the need and function of Eastern studies, and in several consistorial addresses and apostolic letters he returns to this favorite subject of his. The Pope founded the Oriental Institute at Rome, he pleaded with the local ordinaries throughout the world to send priests to Rome to pursue Eastern studies, and he encouraged Catholic universities to create special chairs for research in Oriental Christianity. The pontiff was convinced that only through study would we remove the obstacles of prejudice and misconceptions, and discover the unity of thought and inspiration, obscured by a difference of mentality, that exists between East and West. In the papal letters we find the hope that we ourselves shall expand our theology by studying the Eastern heritage and become enriched as we examine the underlying harmony between the Eastern and Western traditions.

Tentatively and carefully, Pius XI went one step further. This great pontiff, continuing the approach of his predecessors, felt free to declare that the reconciliation between East and West would be beneficial to the entire Catholic Church as well as to the Eastern dissidents. Before this time, such a view had never been admitted. Previously, the advantages of unity envisaged in the Roman documents were all for the separated Eastern Churches. But Pius XI carefully, and Pius XII openly, saw the blessings unity would furnish the whole Catholic Church, East and West. "From the full and perfect unity of all Christians the Mystical Body of Christ and all its members, one by one, are bound to reap great spiritual profits." These are the words of Pius XII in his encyclical *Orientales Omnes*. Catholics too are in need of perfect unity.

This brief survey of papal attitudes toward the Eastern Churches during the last seventy years shows a most remarkable evolution. It would be quite wrong to suppose that this is simply an adoption of new diplomatic techniques. The change of attitude is, rather, based on a deeper insight into the gospel of Christ and its implications in our century. It is based on a deeper understanding of the conditions of grace outside the visible boundaries of the Church, of the universal dimensions of Christian charity, of the implication of the Catholic community in the sin of the world, and of the mysterious character of the Church's unity, which is both perfect and perfectible.

Do we find a similar evolution in the papal attitude toward the Protestant Christians of the West? In this case the problem is rather different. I do not have to emphasize that Protestant Christians, however faithful they may be to their understanding of the gospel, are as a group much further removed from the Catholic Church than are Orthodox Christians. I simply take for granted at this point that Protestant Christians, of whatever Church, are not united by ecclesiastical and sacramental structures as are the Eastern Churches. Protestants have not, moreover, retained the ancient creeds with the faultless fidelity we find in the Eastern traditions. When Protestants believe in Christ as God and Savior, and are baptized in water and the Holy Spirit, they are truly our brethren in the Lord. But as a group, as a community bound by their own Church organization, they are quite far removed from us. It is no wonder, then, that the attitudes of the popes to Protestants are rather different from the full appreciation they have for Eastern Christianity.

Taking this for granted, we observe, nevertheless, a remarkable evolution in the approach to Protestants on the part of recent popes. This development has been much slower than the one discussed above, and it will never take on the same proportions. But a development exists, and it is remarkable enough.

Leo XIII tried to find new ways of speaking and dealing with Protestant Christians. He addressed a number of letters to the Christians of England, of Scotland, and of Germany. With the politeness and charity characteristic of the great Pope, he avoided the insulting vocabulary of the past. He never spoke to them, or of them, as heretics.While it was during his pontificate that Anglican orders were solemnly declared invalid, Leo sought, in carefully guarded statements, to acknowledge the Christian elements in Protestant beliefs, and, especially in his letters to England and Scotland, to express his appreciation of their holiness. Of the English he writes, "The highest credit is due to those who fearlessly and unceasingly proclaim the rights, the laws, and the charter of God almighty and his Son, Jesus Christ," and of the Scottish he says, "Many of these separated Christians love the name of Christ from their heart, endeavor to obey his rule of life, and by imitation seek to follow his holy example." These

are astounding sentences when we compare them with the tone
and tenor of earlier Roman documents.

Leo XIII's desire for unity included the Protestant world. He
initiated and fostered several movements of prayer for unity,
encouraged dissident Christians to pray with us for the fulfillment
of Christ's will in this regard, and sought formulas expressing the
aim of unity which would be suitable to Catholics and Protestants
alike. Most frequently he simply referred to "the great good of
Christian unity" as the object of prayer and endeavor of all believing Christians.

At the same time Leo XIII looked upon Protestantism as a
destructive movement. He considered it as the root of all the un-
rest and upheavals in European society. He spoke on this subject in many of his letters. For him the proper principle of Protestant religion was "private judgment," and he believed that
when this wedge of rationalism was inserted into the divine religion of Christianity, it provoked a multiplication of denominations, the decay of true religion, and the disappearance of faith
in the divine Savior. The Pope believed that all ills, the various
currents of rationalism, secularism, materialism, and socialism
were ultimately due to the first revolt against the sacred unity of
faith in the Western world. Very few Catholic writers of our
own day would be tempted to follow such an interpretation of
European history.

When reading these severe judgments by Leo XIII, we must
not forget that the Protestantism the Pope had in mind was the
religion of higher criticism and of the liberalism of men such as
Harnack. Those were the dreary days of Protestantism, prior to
the ecumenical movement, prior to Karl Barth, form criticism and
neo-orthodoxy, prior to the liturgical and theological renewal of
our own generation.

The attitude of the papacy to Protestantism remained rather
negative for a long time after the reign of Leo XIII. In 1928 Pope
Pius XI felt obliged to condemn the Protestant ecumenical move-

ment. The encyclical *Mortalium Animos* not only forbade
Catholic participation, and sympathy, with the young movement;
it also accused the movement itself of being founded on error
and illusion and hence bound to fail or, at least, do harm to the
cause of truth. Pius XI accused the movement of a "pan-Christian"
inspiration, a desire to reach Christian unity by compromise,
by agreeing to a creed and practices based on the lowest common
denominator of the creeds and practices of existing Churches.
We must admit that Pius could have cited many Protestant
authors who expressed their hopes in these very terms, especially
in the Life and Work movement; but already at that time, there
were other Christians, committed to a creed, orthodox and
sacramental in outlook, more deeply engaged in an authentic
movement for Christian unity. But it was too early for them to
be recognized.

In the official Roman documents, the evolution of an ecumenical outlook in regard to Protestants begins with Pius XII. In his
first encyclical, *Summi Pontificatus,* a new note is sounded. A
single sentence reveals a new approach. With unprecedented
friendliness the Pope acknowledges the good will of the Protestant world. "We cannot pass over in silence the profound impression of heartfelt gratitude made on us by the good wishes
of those who, though not belonging to the visible body of the
Catholic Church, have given noble and sincere expression to
their appreciation of all that unites them to us, in love for the
person of Christ or in belief in God." In this encyclical, and in
countless letters, speeches, radio talks, and other documents,
Pius XII seeks a new way, inspired by Christian charity, of
communicating with Protestant Christians.

The constant reference to Protestants as "separated brethren"
or "separated sons" is remarkable enough, since it acknowledges
what the older ecclesiastical documents were not so willing to
take for granted: the good will on the part of dissident Christians. According to Catholic doctrine, a person rejecting the

faith of the Church with full knowledge of the Church's divine mission, cuts himself off from the source of life. Such a person is a heretic. Such a person no longer has true, supernatural faith in his heart. In the writings of Pius XII, however, it is constantly assumed that the great number of Protestant Christians are outside the Church without guilt, that is, that they are not heretics, but separated brethren. They have faith in God and his Son Jesus Christ. Never before has this point been made clear in papal documents. Protestants are our brothers as Christians. They have access to faith. Though their creed be curtailed and their convictions partial, they have access to God's self-revelation in the Word and his baptism in the Spirit. Receiving these gifts in faith and total commitment, they are truly reborn in Christ, Christians, our brethren, though separated from the Church.

The insight that Protestant Christians have access to real faith, to the faith which justifies, has been implicit in the principles of Catholic theology at all times. Strangely enough, it had hardly ever been clearly acknowledged. In the writings of the great converts of the last century, such as Newman and Manning, who remembered their own states of mind in the faith of their youth, we find this doctrine stated in all clarity; but the great majority of theology manuals and treatises on faith were silent about this question, or only briefly referred to the matter in a footnote. Many Catholics believed, and perhaps still believe, that the gift of faith, by which we cling to God and are justified by him, is not open to men outside the Catholic Church. This is the background against which we must measure the tremendous importance of Pius XII's new emphasis. Protestant Christians are our separated brethren, they are united to us by faith in God and Jesus Christ.

A few weeks before the Second Assembly of the World Council of Churches at Evanston in 1954, Pius XII in a letter to the Augustinian Order, alluding to the dissident ecumenical movement, recalls the moving words St. Augustine had once addressed to men outside the Church seeking Christ's gift of unity: "May those be angry with you who do not know with how much anguish truth is sought; . . . I find it impossible to be angry with you."

This new approach gave the Pope a more sympathetic understanding of the ecumenical movement. He began to realize that a return to the unity willed by Christ is a gift which must be prepared with wisdom. The return to unity is a process of sociological and theological changes which are advanced not so much by individual conversions as by the change of climate, theological dialogue, creative research, and dedicated prayer. The way to unity is gradual. Thus the Pope began to speak of "the journey" toward unity and to express the hope that the Christian society may be led "more and more" to the unity which was lost.

It was during the pontificate of Pius XII that the important Instruction "On The Ecumenical Movement" was published by the Holy Office in 1949. This is in many ways a remarkable document. When it is read thirteen years later, it appears much less positive and encouraging than when it was published. But it must be remembered that this was the first Roman document acknowledging the holiness of the world-wide ecumenical movement, and encouraging Catholics to take a part in it, even if the Church would not participate in the World Council. It is true that the praise of the movement was somewhat guarded, that the co-operation of Catholics was recommended with some reserve; but against a background of perpetual refusals, characteristic of the preceding decades, the Instruction was a great step forward.

The Instruction "On The Ecumenical Movement" permitted Catholics, with the approval of their bishop, to participate in theological dialogue with Protestant Christians. This was an official recognition of the ecumenical movement within the Catholic Church. It is true that the Instruction is more concerned with limiting the movement than with expanding it. Yet, despite the rather guarded tone and the many warnings against the dangers accompanying the movement, the Holy See acknowledged a movement within the Church dealing with Protestants on the basis of a dialogue among equals. The Instruction, we might say, recognizes the movement by defining its limits. It is to be hoped that before long a new and more ample document guiding the Catholic ecumenical movement will be given to us.

It is significant to recall that the Instruction permitted ecumenical gatherings to be opened and closed with prayer in common. Again this was new. In the past the interpretation of ecclesiastical legislation forbidding active Catholic participation in the worship of other Christians, had often been interpreted in the sense that Catholics could never pray with dissident Christians. In this respect the Instruction introduced a more generous attitude.

There is another point contained in the Instruction which must be mentioned in this context. Never before had there been any stress on Protestant studies in the official documents of the Holy See. Pius XI had made such a plea in favor of Oriental studies, but nothing had ever been said in favor of research on the various trends in Protestant theology. In the Instruction we learn that bishops should "bestow their special attention" on the ecumenical movement in their dioceses, and "appoint suitable priests" to study all matters concerning the relationship of Catholics and Protestants.

During the pontificate of Pius XII the attitude of the Holy See toward Protestantism underwent a rapid evolution. Believing Protestants were acknowledged as separated brethren, their ecumenical movement was appreciated as a work of the Holy Ghost, the Catholic ecumenical movement was approved, permission was granted for prayer in common, and Protestant studies received a new encouragement.

Pope John XXIII has advanced the change of attitude even further. Through his personality, his speeches, and especially through the convocation of a General Council, he has created what has been called a new atmosphere in the Church. The Pope affirmed the ecumenical outlook of his predecessors toward the Christians of East and West, and, more especially, he imitated the cordial tone of Pius XII toward Protestants and extended the principles of dialogue with them. There are two points in particular which characterize Pope John's remarkable contribution to the evolution of present-day Catholic ecumenism.

In the first place, John XXIII has spoken out before Protestants, as Pius XI had done before the Orthodox, confessing the Catholic share of responsibility for our unhappy division. This attitude of humility and repentance is of the utmost importance, and we shall have occasion to study its full significance further on. In our century Catholic theologians in dialogue with Protestants have often been impatient with a certain tendency in official documents to defend the Church at all costs, even when to do so meant covering up the deeds of the past or closing one's eyes to present realities. These theologians had desired to admit in all humility that we Catholics are also guilty, that our sins, negligences, and lukewarmness have contributed to the tragic situation in which we find ourselves. Yet since there had never been any official encouragement of such an attitude, they hesitated to confess their repentance in public. Pope John XXIII, in at least two talks, given on January 30, 1959, and September 11, 1960, declared that the Church has made mistakes in the past and that the responsibility for our disunity is divided. "We do not wish to put anyone in history on trial: we shall not seek to establish who was right and who was wrong. Responsibility is divided. We only want to say: let us come together, let us make an end of our divisions."*

The response to these words among Catholics has been remarkable. Bishops in all parts of the world have imitated the Pope in admitting with humility and repentance our involvement in the evils of Christian disunity.

* *Herder-Korrespondenz*, 13 (1959–60), 274.

The second new aspect of Pope John's approach to the problem of Christian disunity is implicit in the convocation of the Second Vatican Council. Let me put it briefly and clearly: according to the Pope, the great contribution of the Catholic Church to the common quest for Christian unity is to seek her own reform. The principle purpose of the Council, we are told, is the renewal of Catholic life and the adaptation of the Church's discipline to the needs of the modern world. The Council will be, in its essence, a Roman Catholic affair. The hope that separated Christians would be invited as participants in a council of the apostolic hierarchy could arise only in people not familiar with the tradition of the Catholic Church. But Pope John has declared on many occasions that it is precisely this renewal of the Church which is her contribution to unity. The Catholic apostolate for Christian unity no longer consists simply in reminding others that they must change: we have been told by the Pope that, for the sake of unity, we too must change.

Reform of the Church, then, is our answer to the divided state of Christianity. We cannot change other people: we can only change ourselves. We cannot make others remove the obstacles which separate us, but we can remove those obstacles to unity for which we ourselves are responsible. In his encyclical *Ad Petri Cathedram,* Pope John declared:

The most pressing topics [of the Council] will be those which concern the spread of the Catholic faith, the revival of Christian standards of morality, and the bringing of ecclesiastical discipline into closer accord with the needs and conditions of our times. This in itself will provide an outstanding example of truth, unity and love. May those who are separated from this Apostolic See, beholding this manifestation of unity, derive the inspiration to seek out the unity which Jesus Christ prayed for so ardently from his heavenly Father.

This is stately language, ponderous and careful, characteristic of all the documents issuing from Rome; but the point is quite clear—the point reiterated in many of the Pope's speeches—that there is ultimately only one thing we can offer our separated brethren in their search for unity: our own reform. It is obvious to any Catholic that there are obstacles to reconciliation which are due to faith itself, based on the revelation of God in Christ; but it is equally obvious that there are many other obstacles which are simply due to the attitudes of men, and can therefore be removed. As Christians we must reduce the distance separating ourselves from one another: as Christians we must seek a greater corporate fidelity to the gospel—and by reforming ourselves we do our part in the movement toward Christian unity.

We have witnessed a remarkable change of attitude toward Christians outside the Church during the decades from Leo XIII to John XXIII. How few the number of years and how great a development! It is no wonder that in many countries Catholics have found it difficult to keep up with this deepening of insight. When we compare the outlook so widespread among us in the past with the present attitude, we see that we have moved from guarded hostility to friendship, from contented ignorance about others to the study of their teachings, from offending them with our terminology to the careful choice of terms expressing our respect, from the suspicion that Protestants are all in spiritual darkness to the conviction that the vast number of them are in good faith, from a distaste for their kind of spirituality to a sympathetic understanding of their aspirations, from an undiscerning justification of our own position to the humble admission that we too are responsible for the division, from the unilateral call for the conversion of others to the realization that we too must change. An enormous evolution, it is true, but one in continuity with Catholic teaching. We believe that the Catholic community is the unique Church of Jesus Christ, the earthly body of the Lord, full of divine grace, a grace which, thank God, is not confined to her borders. This change is not based on fickleness or compromise of principle, but on a deeper insight into the mystery of our redemption in the Church. The change does not belittle the visible, hierarchical Church, or decrease our attachment to her; on the contrary, it is born of an ardent love of the Church and the presence of Christ within her.

3

THE DIVISION OF THE KINGDOM

THE NEW TESTAMENT gives ample witness that the Church is a
people in this world, visibly and socially united. Until fairly recently, this fact was generally denied by Protestant writers. There
was a tendency among them to claim that the Church of Christ
was one only spiritually, that she had never been united in an
historical fashion, not even at the time of the apostles. Today,
however, the great majority of Protestant and Catholic scholars
agree that the community of the apostles, the Church of God
on earth, was united in charity and obedience, in sacramental
practice, and in the confession of the same Lord and Savior.

The polemical concern which tempted Protestants to deny the
historical unity of the Church in the past also tempted Catholic
writers to belabor this very point. They tried to find in the New
Testament a Church united, organized, and governed very much
as we have it in the Church today. They created the impression
that all elements of modern Church life already existed in New
Testament times. Modern biblical scholarship has shown that the
Church was still in a state of transformation at the time of the
apostles, that its visible unity was not clearly defined, that it
remained flexible, protected by charisms and special gifts. Its
organizational unity was just in its beginning stage. The juridical
unity of the various branches of the Church in the days of the

New Testament consisted in the dependence of each community on an apostle and the unity of all the apostles in a closely knit body, the *collegium apostolorum*. The New Testament regards any kind of division threatening the unity of love as a great crime. We know that the words "heresy" and "schism" as found in the New Testament do not yet have their modern, technical meaning; they refer to the tendencies in various local communities to form factions for social reasons, such as in Corinth, or for religious reasons, such as in Ephesus. The apostles act and speak with utmost severity when it is a question of protecting the unity of the Church. The Christian community, according to them, must be one in charity since it constitutes Christ's body on earth. It must be one, moreover, to manifest the newness of life to the world of unbelievers. Division was equated with sin. Already in Galatians "factions and parties" are called works of the flesh, that is, human actions inspired by malice hostile to the Spirit. In the Pastoral Epistles, where we find a more evolved notion of Church unity and ecclesiastical obedience, sins against this holy unity are described in juridical language and judged with the greatest severity. "Avoid a factious man after a first and second admonition, knowing that such a one is perverted and sins; he condemns himself" (Tit 3:11).

The clear antithesis between unity and division which we find throughout the New Testament does *not*, therefore, help us to understand the much later problem of our divided Christianity. The Church learns from the Bible that she must not compromise in the things of the gospel and that separation is a terrible thing, against the will of Christ and his Spirit. It requires strong faith to learn again and again from the New Testament, against all temptations of modern broad-mindedness, that we cannot preserve truth and charity if, even for the sake of human kindness, we become guilty of the slightest infidelity in regard to the apostolic tradition. As truth is not divine if it is without charity, so charity is without essence if it sacrifices truth.

Apart from this clear antithesis between unity and division, the New Testament does not seem to give us much insight into the meaning of schisms and the ruptures of faith. The one reason for factions given in the Scriptures is really an explanation of every evil permitted by God among men: it is a divine trial. St. Paul writes, "There must be factions so that those who are approved may be made manifest among you" (1 Cor 11:19). Divisions for St. Paul are an unqualified evil. There is no attempt to understand their function in history. No clue is given as to what provokes schisms within the Church. They are described simply in terms of human malice. And the reason for this is obvious: since we are dealing with the first generations of Christians in the New Testament, we cannot expect to find anything that resembles the modern problem of Christians, heirs of distinct and divergent traditions. In the Bible, we do not find Christians separated from the Church without guilt.

Can we learn anything in the Bible about the meaning of our present situation? There is *one* schism in the New Testament which might possibly shed some light on Christians divisions: the schism in Israel produced by Jesus Christ. "Behold, this child is destined for the fall and for the rise of many in Israel and for a sign that shall be contradicted" (Luke 2:34). Confronted by the message of Christ, the Jewish people were divided. Some were for him, others against him. On the one hand, we have the establishment of the Church of Jerusalem as a community of Jewish Christians, and, on the other, we hear of the hostility of the Jewish leaders and the persecution they instigated among the people. Is it possible, we ask, to learn anything about divisions in the Christian Church from the schism in the old people of God? Is there perhaps a similarity of divine economy in regard to unity and separation in Israel?

Because of the unity of the divine plan of salvation as expressed in Old and New Testament, we find that the great events in the spiritual history of Israel have significance for the life of the Church under the perfect covenant. We cannot afford to disregard the divine interventions in the Old Testament, imagining that they have nothing to teach us in the age of fulfillment that is ours in the Church of Christ.

Thus led back to the history of Israel, our attention is immediately drawn to a great schism that has preoccupied the minds of the prophets and sacred authors: the schism between the kingdom of Juda (Jerusalem), and the kingdom of Israel (Samaria). This schism, which we shall describe in some detail further on, was always understood as a symbol of Israel's sin and her need of redemption, and, consequently, as a wound that would be healed in the messianic age. "When that time comes, Juda and Israel will be united: together they will come back from the north country to the land I gave your fathers for their home" (Jer 3:18). "As one people, Juda and Israel shall be rallied, under a leader of their common choice" (Os 1:11). "A message from the Lord God! I mean to recall the sons of Israel from their exile among the Gentiles, gather them from every side and restore them to their home. And there, in the hill country of Israel, I will make one nation of them, with one king over them all: no longer shall they be two nations under two crowns" (Ez 37:21). There is no doubt, then, that the schism between the two kingdoms has a special significance in the history of salvation. Let us look at the biblical account of its beginning.

Following the divine will, David founded a single kingdom embracing the twelve tribes of Israel. Together the tribes shared in the covenant, together they were the people of the Lord, together they were to live henceforth in a single kingdom ruled by David, the holy king. God had promised that the throne of David would stand forever. The offspring of David, sitting on the throne of Israel, was to be ruler of the entire world.

Yet we read in the Scriptures that Solomon, David's son, proved disloyal to the God of the covenant. He oppressed his subjects and imitated the potentates of other nations. He constructed for himself an elaborate capital and eventually fell into the worship of foreign gods. Then God intervened. Even before the death of King Solomon, God announced the division of the kingdom.

We read that Jeroboam, one of the leaders of the northern tribes, while walking in an open field met the prophet Ahias clad in a new mantle. They were alone. Then Ahias performed a symbolic action. He took his coat, tore it up into twelve pieces, and bade Jeroboam take ten of them. "This is the message the Lord of Israel sends thee," he said. "I mean to wrest the kingship from the power of Solomon, and make over ten tribes to thee" (3 Kings 11:31). The prophet explained that this will not happen in Solomon's lifetime; but after Solomon's death his son shall see his kingdom divided. The ten tribes of the north shall be severed from Jerusalem. They would form a kingdom of their own. The kingdom of the south, centered on the holy city of Jerusalem, would contain only one tribe, Juda. Though reduced in power and challenged by a rival kingdom in the north, Jerusalem would remain the chosen seat of promise. God would not forget his servant David.

Jeroboam believed the message. He began to act like the king of the north and the declared enemy of Solomon. Yet, since the latter was still in power and had the army on his side, Jeroboam had to flee to Egypt to wait for the proper moment to return.

Then Solomon died. The approximate year given in our history books in 931 B.C. Roboam, his son, was the successor to the throne.

We read in Scripture how Roboam went to Sichem to meet the twelve tribes gathered in assembly in order to be recognized by them and crowned their king. All Israel was present. Even Jeroboam had come back from his refuge in Egypt. On this occasion the northern tribes complained to Roboam. "Thy father," they said to him, "made us bear a bitter yoke. That cruel sway of his, that hard yoke, do thou mitigate, and we will be thy servants on that condition" (3 Kings 12:4). The heir of Solomon hesitated. He asked for two days of deliberation. First he asked advice of the older counselors who had worked with his father for many years. They advised him to give in. "If thou dost defer to them and do their will, granting this request of theirs and speaking graciously to them, they will never cease giving thee loyal service" (3 Kings 12:7). But Roboam turned to his own young friends for counsel, and their advice, contrary to the previous, was more according to his own liking. They said, "Do these people complain that thy father laid a heavy yoke on them, and ask for relief? Then tell them there is more strength in thy little finger than in all the breadth of thy father's back; if his yoke fell heavy on them, thine shall be heavier still; if thy father's weapon was the lash, thine shall be the scorpion." (3 Kings 12:10–11).

On the third day King Roboam met again with all Israel in Sichem, and he told them his decision: "If my father's yoke fell on you heavily, mine shall be heavier still." The king refused to listen to his subjects. He did not recognize the legitimacy of their complaints. He was not concerned with justice; all he desired was power.

But the kingdom of Israel was in the hands of God. He, the Lord of history, now fulfilled the promise he had made to Jeroboam through the mouth of Ahias. He permitted the schism in Israel.

We read that the tribes of the north had their answer ready for King Roboam. "David is none of ours," they cried (3 Kings 12:16). They protested that they had nothing to do with Jerusalem, the throne of David and his city. "Go back, men of Israel, to your homes!" was their cry. The tribes of the north withdrew into their own territory. They seceded from the power of the legitimate ruler. Only the tribe of Juda recognized Roboam as king.

The twelve tribes of Israel were now divided. There were now two kingdoms: the kingdom of the south under Roboam, the heir of David's throne, ruling over the tribe of Juda (and a little later also over Benjamin), and the kingdom of the north made up of ten tribes under Jeroboam, who became their king. Henceforth, the Bible speaks of the kingdom of Juda and the kingdom of Israel.

Immediately after the revolt and secession, a most significant event took place. In Jerusalem, Roboam mustered a whole army to make war on the kingdom of the north. He wanted to repair the schism by force. But again God intervened. He sent the prophet Semeias to the king forbidding him to settle the matter with arms, and to start a war among brothers. "You are not to march out, the Lord says, and make war upon the sons of Israel, your own brethren; go home, every man of you, for this is my doing" (3 Kings 12:24). This schism was God's own doing! Not that God was in favor of dividing the kingdom of promise. But since the royal heir of David's throne had been unfaithful, God permitted the schism by way of punishment and as a step, incomprehensible to men, toward healing the very infidelity which was its cause.

Already at this point we see that in the schism between north and south, there are certain obvious analogies to later schisms in the Church. So far, it must be noted, however, that the rupture between north and south had a purely political and social character. Religious elements, however, were soon to be added. Jeroboam feared that a continued religious association with the Temple at Jerusalem might endanger the independence of his new kingdom. He said to himself, "The kingdom will go back to the dynasty of David if these subjects of mine are allowed to go and sacrifice in the Lord's house at Jerusalem" (12:26). So he built temples in his own territory. "Jeroboam made shrines on the hilltops, and chose men to be priests here and there and everywhere among the people, men that were not of Levi's race" (12:31). These measures, however, were in direct contradiction to the will of God. Jerusalem alone had been singled out as the place of worship (at least according to one biblical tradition) and the house of Levi alone had been chosen to give priests to the nation. The action of Jeroboam was the establishment of a religious schism which offended against the divinely appointed authority of Jerusalem and, soon afterward, opened the door to unorthodox practices and pagan superstitions. The schism which began as a political conflict shattered the religious unity of the people and those who lived in secession lost the protection of Jerusalem and eventually the purity of their faith.

But the story and its moral are not finished at this point. The kingdom of Juda was the true heir of the divine promises. It alone constituted the people faithful to the Lord. The kingdom of the north had cut itself off from the community of salvation. The ten tribes of the north lived outside of the divinely established borders. And yet—this is the important point—the people of the north continued to be brothers of the people of the south. Many of them preserved their faith in the Lord of Israel and their hope in the divine covenant. We read in the Scriptures that despite the state of separation, the Spirit of God continued to act in the ten tribes of the north. Prophets kept on appearing in the north, sent by the Lord to deliver their messages to the people. Elias and Elisha were from the north. Later we find Osee. God had not forgotten his separated people; he remained with them, although he condemned their schism. He did not cease sending them messengers recalling them to greater holiness and fidelity to the covenant.

While the promises and legitimacy were all on the side of the kingdom of Juda, this did not necessarily guarantee the holiness of its people. On the contrary, conscious of the divine promise in regard to the Temple at Jerusalem, the people were constantly tempted to be complacent, to "take things easy," and to neglect the obligations of their faith. They believed that nothing could happen to them since they had the Temple of the Lord in their midst. They did not always recognize that the heritage of things divine is a source of life only if we acknowledge and endorse them by a personal decision. It was especially the task of the prophets to stir up the people, to make them see the holiness of God and the selfishness of their own ways. And we must add: the prophets of the north were also called to utter God's word to the kingdom of the south. Their role was not confined to the north; their message had a special meaning for the south. It was meant to stir up the people of the south, to drive out their smugness and self-satisfaction, their easy trust in the legitimacy of their position; they were to be reminded that God desires a loyalty which is total.

The division of the two kingdoms presents a certain analogy to the events that produced our divided Christianity. A schism occurs which is basically due to the sin of man. If the leadership in the south had been more enlightened and more responsible, the division could have been avoided. Even though eventually the greatest difference between north and south was the religious question, in the beginning it was political and social factors which created the tensions and caused the rift. The first answer of the south to the sudden revolt was the mustering of an army in order to obtain national unity by force. But God intervened: no force must be used. This division is God's doing. Not, as we have seen, that God desired the separation of the two kingdoms. But it was he who had decreed the punishment and who had planned purification and final victory through the sad events of the separation.

It is unfortunate that the divine condemnation of force has not always been understood in the history of the Christian Church. Again and gain we have been tempted to heal the breaches and rifts among Christians by the use of military power and political manipulations; in fact, we have often tried it, and it has never been successful. God saw to that.

The schism of the kingdom did not divide the people into groups having equal shares. On the contrary. Only the south remained attached to the seat of authority, the Temple of Jerusalem and the throne of David. Only the south was in the strict sense the people of God and the community of salvation. The people who left the unity of David's realm may have been provoked by injustices on the part of the king, they may have been less guilty in terms of personal responsibility than the king himself and especially his evil advisers, but the fact remains that it was they, the northerners, who were outside the authentic realm of God's promise. Is there not here a true analogy to the Christians of the north who left the Catholic Church for reasons which may have appeared justified to them and which were in part provoked by faults and crimes of Catholic leadership? Yet here also the fact remains: whatever may be said regarding the motives, Protestant Christians have cut themselves off from the true Church of Christ; they are visibly outside the one community of salvation.

At the same time, even if collectively the tribes of the north had left the community of God's promise, individually they were still open to the influence from above. As a group, they were outside, but the Holy Spirit continued to act in the hearts of the people. Is not this somewhat the Protestant situation, or at least one element of it? Protestants do not constitue the Church, or even part of the Church. Collectively we must say that they have no claim on the divine promises. But individually they may possess the Holy Ghost. God continues to work in their hearts. They remain our brothers in spite of the separation; they belong in some very real sense to the family which is the Church.

We know from history that the Spirit continues to raise up prophets in the midst of Protestants reminding them of greater fidelity to God. And may we not go further? Must we not admit that as the ancient prophets of the north had a message also for the south, so it is in our own age? Is it not possible that God wishes to remind us through the preaching and criticism of northern prophets of the aspects of truth we have neglected? God corrects and chastises us by the forces of history which he controls. Is there nothing that God wants to teach us through Luther or Calvin? Is there no message of God addressed to us in

Kierkegaard, Karl Barth, in the World Council of Churches? We need ears of faith to recognize and acknowledge the prophetic voices coming to us from our separated brethren of the north. If we are humble enough to realize that we are only partially faithful to the infinite riches of Catholic truth, then we know that we have much to learn and are in constant need of being reminded of that fact.

How did the prophets of the south look upon the kingdom of the north? They acknowledged its painful separation from the community of the promise. At the same time, they recognized the authentic, prophetic voices of the north. More than that, in judging the people of their age, the prophets of Juda were much more severe with their own people than with the separated brothers from the north. Jeremias exclaims, "The rebellious Israel [of the north] has justified her soul, in comparison with the treacherous Juda [of the south]" (3:11), and Ezechiel announces, "Samaria [of the north] has not committed half thy sins; thou [Juda] hast surpassed them with thy crimes and hast justified thy sisters by all the abominations thou hast committed" (16:51). Precisely because the kingdom of Juda was the legitimate heir of the divine promises, did the sins of its people count more heavily against them. The greater the truth and the more abundant the means of grace, the more terrible also is the weight of sin.

This is a principle which is true also today, though it has not usually determined the attitudes of Catholics toward those separated from them. If we claim to be the true Church of Christ in which the fullness of his gifts is available to us, surely our own infidelities count much heavier against us than do the sins among separated Christians. If they have less light, their excuse is better. If we have more grace, our guilt is greater.

As a rule, our attitude is really the very opposite. We have a tendency to find all kinds of excuses for our own failings, but tend to be strict with others. The bigotry of Protestants annoys us very much, but the bigotry in our own midst we consider a natural by-product of fervor. The prejudice, the distortions, and the many failings against love which our Protestant brethren commit against us, provoke us to great anger; but our own failings against charity in regard to them we hardly notice at all. We are sometimes tempted to feel that because we are right and they wrong, we are dispensed from subjecting our attitude toward them to the strict canon of charity. We apply standards to them which we do not keep ourselves.

The attitude of the prophets was the very opposite. The greater the insight, the greater also moral responsibility. And this is in harmony with authentic Catholic theology. If we claim to be the one true Church of Christ, surely we must weigh our acts in more refined scales than those of other people.

We conclude, then, that the Bible does throw some light on the problem of our divided Christendom. The New Testament offers us the single message that the Church of Christ is indestructibly one and that divisions among Christians are tantamount to sin. But, reading the two Testaments together, we discover that there is a message for our modern problem of Christians divided not by choice but by heritage.

It is in fact rewarding from our viewpoint to consider a little further the consequences of the schism between Juda and Israel. We learn from the Scriptures that the heirs and successors of the northern tribes were the Samaritans. After the destruction of the northern kingdom, a considerable part of the people remained in the area and intermingled with the pagan population. Owing to these pagan influences, the religion of the north suffered further deterioration. It seems that Yahveh, the God of the patriarchs, became for the people a national deity to whom other gods from neighboring communities were added. At the same time there must have been purifying influences at work among the Samaritans. They did keep the Pentateuch, the five books of Moses, as the inspired Scripture. At the time of our Lord, at any rate, the Samaritans had rejected polytheism and idolatry. They believed in the God of their fathers and expected the coming of the promised messias.

The hostility between Jews and Samaritans after the exile is well known. The Old Testament gives witness to the mutual hatred between the two peoples. We learn that when the Jews returned from Babylon to establish themselves in Jerusalem, a group of Samaritans wished to join them; but they were rejected. We also learn that the Samaritans tried to hinder the rebuilding of the temple and the construction of the city walls in Jerusalem. Because the Samaritans were so close to the Jews, both ethnically and in terms of their faith, they were often detested with more passion than were the pagan nations. They regarded one another as schismatics or heretics. We know that there was no social intercourse between the two groups. At the time of our Lord, the Jews would go out of their way to avoid passing through the land of the Samaritans. This custom was certainly followed by Jesus and his family, except on one occasion, as we shall see, when Jesus purposely traversed Samaria.

Do we not have in the strained relationship between Jews and Samaritans a certain analogy to the division within Christendom? In the past we have often avoided one another, we have often had greater dislike for one another than for godless and non-Christian men. Looking upon one another as heretics or schismatics, we felt religiously justified in not seeking any bond of charity at all. It is therefore of greatest practical importance for us to know what Christ's attitude was to the Samaritans. Did he approve of the exclusiveness of his own people? Did he encourage their animosity toward the Samaritans, or did he try to break down the traditional barriers between the two peoples?

Our Lord did not regard the Samaritans as Jews. For him they did not belong to the chosen people. Sending his disciples on their first mission, he told them, "Do not go in the directions of the Gentiles, nor enter the towns of Samaritans, but go to the lost sheep of the house of Israel" (Matt 10:5). Only after his victory on the cross did the Lord send his disciples as witnesses "in Jerusalem and in all Judea, in Samaria, and even to the ends of the earth" (Acts 1:8). This latter quotation shows that Jesus and his followers regarded the Samaritans as separated from Israel and yet, in some way, as belonging to it. They were neither Jews nor Gentiles. They belonged to a category by themselves.

This peculiar position is well brought out in the fourth chapter of John's Gospel where we read of Jesus' encounter with the Samaritan woman. When Christ asks her for a drink of water, she is surprised: "How is it that thou, although thou art a Jew, dost ask drink of me, who am a Samaritan woman? Jews do not associate with Samaritans." The woman recognized that the social separation between her people and Jesus' was complete. The mutual contempt between the two groups was an attitude which had become natural. When the Pharisees, according to the same Gospel, were disturbed by what appeared to them as unorthodox and subversive ideas, they asked Jesus, "Art thou a Samaritan?" (8:48). All this the woman recognizes and she is amazed that Jesus simply breaks the age-old reserve.

In the course of the conversation, the woman recalls the difference between Jews and Samaritans, mentioning both their similarity and their distance from one another. We too worship God, the woman says, we worship him on this mountain, while the Jews claim that he must be worshipped at Jerusalem. The Samaritan temple on Mount Gerizim had been constructed at the time of Nehemias, in direct opposition to the Temple rebuilt at Jerusalem. The Samaritan sanctuary had been destroyed in 128 B.C. by the Jewish king and high priest John Hyrcanus, but the mountain remained sacred to the people. From other sources we know that the Samaritans accepted the Pentateuch, while they rejected the consequent revelations made to Israel. They did, however, believe in the coming of the messias. To this the woman gives clear witness: "I know that the messias is coming, and when he comes he will tell us all things."

At the same time, Jesus insists on the difference between the Jews and the Samaritans. He identifies himself with the religious mission of his people. "We worship what we know," he says, "while you worship what you do not know. Salvation is from the Jews." What does this mean? Is Jesus here denying that the Samaritans worship the God of Israel, the Lord of the covenant? After all, they did regard themselves as Israelites, and even if they were then living in schism, they did not abandon their trust in the covenant. When Christ claimed that they worship what they do not know, he did not deny any knowledge of God, in the modern, philosophical sense, among the Samaritans. "To know" God means here to live in harmony with the entire will of the Lord, and this the Samaritans were unable to do outside of the worship of God at Jerusalem.

In the same conversation, Jesus announces the end of an era. "The hour is coming when neither on this mountain nor in Jerusalem will you worship the Father. . . . The hour is coming, and is now here, when you will worship the Father in spirit and in truth." Jesus foretells a new era when all men, independent of their origin, even beyond the election of Israel, will have access to God in a more direct and intimate fashion because they shall have been born of the Spirit (3:3–8) and sanctified by the word of truth (17:17, 19). Because men shall be made sons of God, there will be a new worship. Because men shall be reborn in the spirit, all differences due to the ancient dispensation will disappear. Salvation comes from the Jews, but in the new age all men shall be one in a sanctified Israel.

The attitude of Jesus to the Samaritans as evidenced in this episode is rather complex. He excludes them from the community of divine worship. Despite their good faith, and despite the large elements of truth they possess, they are considered outsiders to the Jewish people. At the same time, the love of Christ goes out to them. He is willing to break the traditional separation. He associates with them. Not only that, he looks upon the Samaritans in the light of the fulfillment about to come, and he sees that, despite their present separation, they are on the way to being united beyond the present schism.

Do we not have here a certain similarity to the Catholic attitude toward separated Christians and, in a more remote sense, to Jews? They are severed from the Catholic community as a group, and we would serve them ill if we tried to dissimulate our differences. At the same time, we are to love them, not only from a distance but through personal contact. Friendship across the religious border is not only possible; it is a holy thing. We must always look at separated Christians and at Jews as ultimately destined to be one with us. For the time will come, and is already coming, when all who are faithful to the gracious will of God shall transcend the divisions and enter into one community. We believe that this community of saints, established in glory on the last day, will be in continuity with the Catholic Church, just as much as the foundation of this Church is in continuity with the Israel of old. But this reunion will not be like the victory of one group over another; it will be the fulfillment of the hopes of all of us.

Approaching the Samaritans in this new way, Jesus discovered great loyalty among them. Thanks to the enthusiastic account of the woman, many of the villagers came out to Jesus and persuaded him to stay with them. Many of them came to believe.

We touch here upon a favorite theme of John and the other evangelists which is in perfect harmony with the attitude of the ancient prophets. To put to shame the Jews, their own people, they would dwell on the virtues of strangers, especially of those whom the Jews tended to despise. We have mentioned this above.

Precisely because Israel was the chosen people and had access to the mercy of God, the loyalty of foreigners was more remarkable and the sin of foreigners more readily excused. "Many will come from the east and from the west, and will feast with Abraham and Isaac and Jacob in the kingdom of heaven, but the children of the kingdom will be put forth into the darkness out-side" (Matt 8:11–12). This and similar prophetic threats had one single purpose: to stir up the people to be converted to their Lord. After Christ had cured ten lepers with miraculous power, we read that only one of them returned to give thanks, and he was a Samaritan. "Has not one been found to give glory to God except this foreigner?" (Luke 17:18) was the reproachful reply of Christ. As a true prophet in Israel, Jesus put to shame his own beloved people.

The charity of a Samaritan has been made proverbial in a parable of the Lord recorded in Luke's Gospel. The parable of the Good Samaritan is well known; but since it is often abstracted from its historical context, we fail to be duly impressed by its message. We must recall above all the tensions and enmity existing between Jews and Samaritans. The Pharisees, with their emphasis on fidelity to the Law and other observances, were especially tempted to despise the schismatics of the north. One of these Pharisees asked Christ: "What is the first commandment?" And Christ, following the teaching of Scripture, answered without hesitation: "To love God and after him your neighbor" (cf. Dt 6:5, Lev 19:18). Charity is the first commandment of divine religion. And yet there was something new about Christ's commandment. Who was this neighbor the people were to love? Was he just a member of their own group? Was he the foreigner living within Israel? Or was this neighbor any and every man in the whole world, whatever his relation to Israel?

In the eyes of the Jewish clergy and the ordinary people in Jerusalem, the charity God demanded of them was often restrictive. They tended to limit their love to Israel alone. The Old Testament, especially in its prophetical books, contains the most outspoken universalist utterances, but the theme had remained rather unemphasized in the religion of the Law as practiced in Jerusalem. But let us not despise the Jews of Jerusalem for this narrowness. We ourselves have much to learn on this score.

Even though a universal and unbounded love is the most central message of the New Testament, Christians have been quite slow in extending their charity to those beyond the pale. Loving our neighbor surely does not mean loving only our Christian neighbor. It means loving the others also. Our charity is not Catholic when it is confined to Catholics.

If we read the parable of the Good Samaritan against this background, we discover that its message is most significant for our day. It is, if I may say so, an ecumenical parable. The stranger lies by the wayside, wounded, unable to move. The first person walking by is a temple priest; but he is not moved to action, he does not come over to offer his help. If the parable were to be translated to fit the present situation, we would have to say that a priest in his car drives past human misery and is not moved. The second person in the parable is a Levite. He saw the wounded stranger and walked past. Translating this into a modern situation, but guarding the evangelical meaning, we would have to make this man a deacon, or a religious, a man who is professionally linked to religious worship. And then comes the Samaritan. Seeing the wounded man, "he is moved with compassion," he comes over, he helps, he cares. He loves. If we want to fit this parable into a modern situation, whom shall we choose to represent this Samaritan? Who plays the part of this heretic from the north? Let us face the accusation contained in the parable. Perhaps a Baptist comes along to give us a lesson in Christian charity.

The reaction of our Lord's audience to this parable must have been one of surprise and perhaps annoyance. Christ taught the universality of love in two ways: first by showing that "my neighbor" whom I must love is simply any man who is in need, and secondly by revealing the unholiness of any restrictive notion of charity which would exclude the heretic or the enemy. The people you despise, our Lord suggested, have a deeper insight into love than you; and hence they are closer to God. The

Pharisee who put the question was so upset by the parable that when asked who proved himself a neighbor, he was unable to pronounce the word: the Samaritan. The distance was still too great. He had to chose a circumlocution: he said instead, "he who had pity on him." He accepted the story, but was he willing to learn from it?

God continues to send Good Samaritans to his Church. God continues to teach us and to put us to shame by raising up men outside the Church who give us an example of holiness. This is a subject to which we must return later. For the moment I only wish to say that it requires grace and humility to discover the Good Samaritan and to receive through him the message from the Lord of the Church.

Reflecting on Jesus' attitude toward the Samaritans, we conclude that it reflects a certain duality. On the one hand they are outside the community of salvation, on the other they may individually be full of divine charity. They are in error objectively, but this does not necessarily exclude them from grace. They constitute an organized religious community which as such cannot be integrated into the structure of true religion, but they are destined to be united to the true Israel in the new age of the Spirit.

The relevance of these remarks to the Catholic attitude toward Protestants is obvious.

At the same time, we must not forget that the Catholic Church is the fulfillment of Israel and the age of preparation to which it belonged. Jesus Christ is the royal heir on David's throne; and with him as head, it is impossible that the messianic community be divided into two separate bodies. While we heard in the Old Testament that God announced the schism in David's realm through a prophet's mantle torn into twelve pieces, we read in the New Testament that "the tunic [of Jesus] was without seam, woven into one piece from the top," and that even the soldiers would not tear it to pieces (cf. John 19:23). The author of the

Fourth Gospel, carrying forward the prophetic symbolism of the Old Testament, proclaims with assurance that, through the glorious death of Christ, a new order of salvation had begun in which the unity of God's people was irrevocable.

The Church is one. We have discussed this unity from one point of view in the first chapter. We regarded unity as that quality of the Church by which the members of the Church are brought together in divine charity and through which all divisions in the world are to be healed. The dynamism of this unity may be stronger or weaker in different ages—this we know from history—but the essential unity of the Church cannot be lost—this we know from the Scriptures. In the Church the peace of Christ has been established once and for all among men.

It is the characteristic of all the New Testament gifts to mankind that they are at one and the same time free gifts to be constantly received and great tasks to be daily achieved. This is true of the whole work of our sanctification. We learn from Catholic teaching that the grace of justification establishes us in holiness with a true permanency, but we are told by the same teaching that the Christian is constantly in need of divine mercy. We are truly holy in grace, yet we are never dispensed from saying, "Lord, have mercy on us." The gift we receive must unceasingly be ratified by an inner conversion.

But what is true of Christ's gift to individuals is also true of the divine equipment bequeathed upon the Church. All is freely given, her unity among the most precious gifts; but all must be daily sought in repentance.

This dynamic aspect of unity has often been overlooked. For apologetical reasons, as noted earlier, we have often defined the Church's unity simply in terms of the external marks which constitute the Church as a visible society of men. The Church is one, we are wont to say, because of the unity of creed, liturgy, government. Even if such a definition appears useful in our arguments with other Churches, it seems logically inadequate, if not incorrect. No external marks can determine, or define, a unity as holy, profound, and supernatural as that of the Church. No social institutions can guarantee the unity which Christ has established in our midst. The unity of the Church must be defined in terms of Christ, or of his Spirit which vivifies her; there is no other guarantee for the permanent nature of this unity than the once-and-for-all victory of the Lord. It is quite true that the unity which Christ gave the Church expresses itself *also* through her social body, her creed, her liturgy, and her apostolic government; but we know that if these elements existed alone, unaccompanied by the grace of the Spirit and the charity they are to generate, the Church would not be *one* in a supernatural sense. The promise that the Church shall remain forever does not simply mean that the social institution shall be permanent, but precisely that this social institution shall always be filled with the Holy Spirit. Creed, liturgy, and apostolic government are means by which Christ creates unity in us. They are not themselves the unity.

This tendency to materialize the notion of the Church seemed quite useful in arguments with Protestants. It made it easy on the one hand to demonstrate that we are the true Church by pointing to the three visible marks not possessed by other communities, and on the other it made the Church appear untouched and untouchable by the secession of protesting Christians from her ranks. By making Church unity a somewhat legal concept, it ceased to be looked upon as a task to be achieved, and the Catholic Church began to appear as an invulnerable quantity in this world.

The ancient Christian writers, looking upon the gifts of Christ as something freely given to be daily ratified, were deeply conscious that the Church's unity, perfectly established in Christ, was something ever to be affirmed and sought in charity. They felt therefore that schism and heresy profoundly wounded the Church of Christ. The heretics and schismatics who cut themselves off from the Catholic Church suffered the greater pain; but the Church herself bore the wounds of disunity in her body too. The severed Christians were never regarded as completely "outside." Since they had been regenerated by holy baptism, their separation from the community reduced the unity in love of those to whom the Church had given new life. Most authors of recent centuries, for apologetical reasons, have ceased to speak of the *vulnera Ecclesiae*. The recent popes, however, occasionally returned to the more ancient way of speaking, which freely admits that disunity of Christians, though not destroying the Church's unity, does inflict grave wounds upon her. Benedict XV once encouraged the labor of Protestants for Christian unity so "that the mystical body of Christ be no longer drawn apart and cut to pieces."

Since Christian unity was also intended by Christ as a sign proclaiming his message of reconciliation, we must humbly admit that our disunity weakens this sign considerably. The Lord prayed, "That they may be one . . . that the world may know that Thou hast sent me" (John 17:21). Here again we have been in the habit for centuries of considering this sign, not as a part of the good news proclaiming Christ's peace, but as a logical element from which to construct a syllogism. We preferred to interpret this sign as the external unity of creed, liturgy, and government, which is always visible and quite untouched by Christian divisions. If we consider these external bonds as means through which Christ communicates himself to us, then this approach is quite legitimate. But it should not blind us to the fact that according to John's Gospel Christian unity is a proclamation of Christ's messianic power to unify mankind and of the Church's mission to embrace all Christians as a single family. Though fully given to the Church in Christ, this unity is imperfect as long as Christians are divided into separated communities. Again, it is our recent popes who have frankly admitted that Christian disunity lessens the preaching power of the Church.

We must conclude, therefore, that despite the irrevocable unity

Christ gave to the Church, there is room in her to speak of a waning and waxing of this unity. As long as this world lasts, the unity of the Church remains something to be achieved. Despite the elevation of the New Testament over the stage of preparation found in the Old, there is still room to apply to the Church, in some analogy, whatever we read of the divisions and lack of unity in regard to the ancient Israel. What we read of the old biblical schism between Israel and Juda has not become altogether inapplicable to the Christian community. In a proper theological perspective, taking into account the sovereign victory of Christ, the imperfections of the ancient Israel still have a message for us.

This is the double character of the divine gift in this world, completely present in Christ and inadequately achieved by us. We live in the tension between "already" and "not yet" which marks the eschatological time of waiting, the little while between Christ's resurrection and his return at the end of time.

4

THE MEANING OF SCHISMS

WE HAVE EXAMINED the Scriptures to gain a deeper understanding of the disunity of Christians from which we suffer. Though it appeared at first as if the New Testament had little to tell us on this score, we found a schism in the Old Testament which brought out some of the characteristics of the divisions in Christendom. We found, in particular, that separated Christians remain in all truth our brethren. The question arises now, What is the meaning of our division? Why does God permit his people to be subject to such afflictions? Why does Christ allow that his followers, his own brethren, those who believe in his resurrection, be disunited in distinct communities?

This is not a theoretical question. We must ask ourselves what God wants to teach us through these divisions. One of the great messages of the Scriptures is that the events of history have a meaning. They reveal the will of God to those who believe; they are God's instruments for the formation of his holy people and the redemption of all mankind. Even though it is impossible to understand the divine intention behind a great number of historical events, it makes sense to ask why gifts as essential to the life of the Church as unity are lost in the upheaval of the ages. If God, the Lord of history, permits schisms which are so contrary to the nature of the Christian community, he must want to reveal something to us through them. The schisms must have a message.

At first glance, as we have already seen, the New Testament does not give us an answer. Divisions among Christians are due to human malice. The one reason given why the Lord permits them is one that is applicable to all evil: for the testing and purification of the elect. "There must be factions," St. Paul writes, "so that those who are approved may be made manifest among you" (1 Cor. 11:19). This applies especially to the time of the apostles when various religious currents passed through the young communities, and holiness and salvation were open only to those who remained loyal to Paul and the apostolic tradition he himself had received. But such a general principle does not permit us to understand the divided state of the Christian world today.

For the moment we must place the problem of why God permits schisms in the Church into a wider context by asking the more general question: Why does God permit that his Church should suffer? Why is the Church vulnerable to persecutions, failures, lukewarmness, divisions, and other calamities? Is she not God's holy people, and is there not a special providence protecting the community of salvation? If the history of the Church is meaningful, we must ask why she is constantly exposed to miseries.

The first answer which we must give to this question is simple and beautiful. As Christ was persecuted and failed in his earthly endeavors, so the Church, following in the footsteps of her Master, also passes through the valley of lowliness and injustice. "No servant is greater than his master. If they have persecuted me, they will persecute you also" (John 15:20). These are the words of Jesus. As he was visited by the hate of the world, so shall his Church be. "If the world hates you, know that it has hated me before you. If you were of the world, the world would love what is its own. But because you are not of the world, but I have chosen you out of the world, therefore the world hates you" (John 15: 18–19). As Christ was holy and thus provoked the anger of evil men, so the Church, due to her holiness, to her defense of the gospel, must arouse the irritation and hatred of the selfish and powerful in the world. The Church is opposed, persecuted, or visited by schisms, we conclude, because she is destined to grow in the likeness of Christ and to convert the world to holiness by her humility, her readiness to suffer, and her loyalty to truth, even at the cost of persecution.

This is one reason, one of several. If we believed that this was the *only* reason for the wounds inflicted upon the Church, we would be led to an unbearable degree of hypocrisy and arrogance. We must acknowledge, alas, that the Church has often been hated because of her identification with a particular social structure or a certain political regime. The Church has sometimes been despised and hindered in the free exercise of her activity because of the partiality, narrowness, and outmoded science which, in certain countries, was offered as her official view. There were times in the past when the Church was persecuted because of the secular power of her bishops, including the popes, and the political associations which such power necessarily established. The reason why the Church is opposed and hated by people in our own century is not always on account of her loyalty to Christ and his gospel, but often because she is accused, rightly or wrongly, of having neglected the poor and their social interests. Must we not admit, therefore, that the reason why Catholics are persecuted is not only because the Church is holy, but also because we are unholy? Is it in harmony with Catholic theology to say that God chastises the Church? This introduces the question of sin in the Church and the theology of her holiness. To understand the meaning of schisms in the Church we must make a digression and look at these aspects of her life.

The Old Testament gives us a detailed doctrine of sin and holiness in Israel. God chose for himself a people which was to be his servant on earth. He established a people which was to worship him and be his instrument in the salvation of all mankind. God confirmed this election in a covenant, promising his guidance and protection and obliging the people to follow his Law, a covenant which was sometimes announced as a bilateral agreement and sometimes as a free divine disposition in regard to Israel. There are a multitude of passages in Scripture which suggest that God has bound himself to the terms of the covenant as long as, and only as long as, Israel is faithful to the Law. There are other passages making it clear that God has really committed himself to the people to such an extent that his merciful designs shall never be altered, whatever the obstacles of human sin.

We find two kinds of divine oracles in the Old Testament. There are messages of the Lord threatening to wipe out the people: "Do not fall away into worship of foreign gods! The Lord thy God who dwells so close to thee, is jealous in his divine love, and if he is roused to anger with thee, he will sweep thee off the face of the earth" (Dt 6:14–15). At the same time the Lord repeatedly declares his eternal love: "Yes, when all these threats have come home to thee, thou wilt turn back to the Lord thy God at last, and listen to his voice. The Lord thy God is a God of mercy; he will not forsake thee, will not utterly destroy thee, and will not forget the sworn covenant he made with thy fathers" (Dt 4:30–31). Both of these messages are true. Both reveal the secret of the divine government. We can watch their application throughout the history of the people of Israel. When Israel was faithful to the terms of the covenant God manifested himself as protector, guide and benefactor, and whenever Israel became unfaithful, and this happened very often, then God remained faithful to his promises not by blessing the people but by chastising them. Reading the Old Testament, we constantly witness the fall of Israel into infidelity, and the punishment to which it was exposed for this. At the same time, with every new fall a new pardoning was announced and after the chastisement the people were taken back into God's mercy. Israel could not lose itself among other nations, despite the multitude of its sins. God remained faithful. By revolting against God, Israel would withdraw from the benefits of the covenant and enter a period of darkness; but the covenant remained firmly established.

This mysterious covenant relationship with Israel, which was both a treaty and a testament, was expressed in a theological dialectic, often in highly poetical terms, carried on throughout the prophetical literature of the Old Testament. On the one hand, Israel (or Jerusalem) was the faithful servant, the beloved son, the throne of God, the holy city, the place of salvation, and, on the other hand, it was also the unfaithful servant, the treacherous son, the stiff-necked people, the city of rebellion. Israel was both simultaneously. It was unfaithful to its Lord; and at the same time it was the dearly beloved of the Lord, faithful to the Lord because of what he did for her.

This theme is expressed a hundred times over in the poetic image of Israel (Jerusalem), the spouse of Yahweh. This image occurs most often in the prophetic threats uttered to the nation. In Jeremias (Chapter 3), Osee (Chapter 2), Ezechiel (Chapter 23) and the Second Isaias, Jerusalem is the unfaithful wife, chosen by God her lover in her youth, cherished by him, protected by him, and yet for all that love, rebellious, treacherous, and wanton. Abandoning the Lord and worshiping foreign gods, Jerusalem commits adultery, she gives herself to other men, runs after them, becomes a harlot. At the same time, however, the identical Jerusalem remains the beloved of her husband, the bride he woos, the spouse he pleads to return, the only woman who will ever please him. The Lord says to her: "False to thy oath, thou hast forsworn our covenant, and thou shalt have the punishment thou hast earned. That covenant I made with thee in thy youth shall not be forgotten, nay, I will ratify it eternally, but humbled thou shalt be with the memories of past days" (Ez 16:59–61). Israel is constantly holy by her election, unholy by her rebellion, and holy again by divine restoration.

Now we may ask the question, Why did God's people in the old dispensation suffer persecution, divisions, and other ills? We know the answer from the Bible. Often Israel was hated and persecuted because it was the people chosen of the Lord, because of its special mission, its worship of the invisible God. Israel had to suffer the anger of the nations because she was holy. At the same time we read that wars, invasions, revolts, and factions were inflicted upon the people, not because they were holy but because they were unholy. These things were meant as punishments, instruments of divine justice and divine mercy, purifying the people and leading them back to their Lord.

Can we transfer this theory of sin and holiness in God's people to the new Israel purchased by the blood of Christ? The answer is No. God's people of the Old Testament belonged to the divine stage of preparation, while God's people of the New Testament are the bearers of the divine fulfillment. What was prophesied in Israel is fulfilled in the Church; what was promised under the Old Law is accomplished under the New. The Church is established in holiness because she is in Christ, in her Lord who has risen once and for all. This, at least, is the first answer we must give, even if we shall see further on that in a certain sense the rhythm of sin, chastisement, and re-entry into grace remains meaningful for God's people in the New Testament.

At this point it is worth mentioning that traditional Protestant theology would answer our question emphatically in the affirmative. For Protestant theologians the Church, like Israel, is irrevocably established in a covenant with God, but like Israel, she is constantly revolting against the Lord and hence in perpetual need of radical reformation. If we read in the Old Testament that God intervened in mercy to punish and pardon his people, these divine interventions, according to Protestant writers, are multiplied without number in the people of the New Testament. God has so committed himself to the Church in Jesus Christ that he constantly pardons her sins and reforms her deviations: and it is precisely in these divine interventions that the holiness of the Church consists. According to such a theology the Church of Christ is indeed holy, because of the new and perfect covenant, but holy with a sanctity which is altogether God's and in no way the Church's own. In a Protestant ecumenical document we read: "In spite of our unholiness, we know that the Church of God is holy, for it is God's action and not our penitence which sanctifies and renews it." In the eyes of Protestant theologians the Church remains susceptible to complete deformation even while she continues to be the place where Christ reveals himself to the world.

Such a theology of the Church is quite unacceptable on the basis of the Catholic creed. For us the situation of the Church in the world is not that of ancient Israel among the nations. The Church is no longer vulnerable by the inadequacies of her members. She has been established beyond infidelity by the victory of her Lord. The Church is in Christ. The crucified and risen Savior shares with his Church the fullness of his holiness. This doctrine is taught clearly and with emphasis by St. Paul, who joyfully announces the pleroma, God's pleroma in the Church.

Pleroma or fullness is a biblical term which is usually applied to God himself. This fullness of God is not the richness of his own unlimited divine resources; it seems, rather, to refer to what is filled by God. In the Old Testament this fullness signifies the universe full of divine creativity and power. The Psalmist sings, *Domini est terra et plenitudo eius* (The Lord's are the earth and its fullness; Ps. 23:1). The prophet Isaias saw the world filled with the glory of the Lord: *Pleni sunt caeli et terra gloria tua*. When St. Paul writes in his Epistle to the Colossians that "It has pleased God that in [Christ] all his fullness should dwell" (1:19), the apostle does not refer to the divine nature which is present in Christ. He already established the divinity of Christ in a preceding sentence (1:15–17), explaining that Christ was associated in the creation of all things. Speaking of the fullness in Christ, the apostle is concerned with another point. He deals with the effects of the redemptive incarnation in Christ and wants to show that in this Christ is present the renewal of the universe. Through his death and resurrection Christ has become the head of a new humanity and the beginning of a new creation. The pleroma of God in Christ is the divine power present in the Savior destined to transform this world, including humanity, according to the redemptive plan of the eternal Father. And hence, after announcing that the pleroma of God dwells in Christ, Paul immediately speaks of the complete restoration of all things in Christ (1:20). The pleroma of God in Christ therefore is the inexhaustible source of this universal reconciliation.

In Christ, Paul teaches us, we have access to the divine pleroma. "For in him [Christ] the pleroma of the Godhead dwells bodily, and in him who is the head of every principality and power, you have received of that pleroma" (Col 2:29). Christ has been made head of the universe, that is, of humanity and the rest of creation, in order to re-establish all things in a new order. Baptized into him and grafted into him by faith, we share in his supernatural life. The divine life he has received to share with the world is to be the new and gratuitous vitality of the redeemed and sanctified.

According to the doctrine of the apostle, however, this pleroma is not simply present in Christ, available to individual believers. The pleroma is, rather, handed over as such to the Church, Christ's body on earth, in which men are to find their new life. The biblical doctrine of redemption is far removed from modern individualistic notions of religion. God's gift to men as announced in the Scriptures is destined to save a people and to redeem the whole human family. Salvation passes to mankind not as a summing up of those who are saved individually. On the contrary, the individual is saved by being drawn into a divine economy established for humanity. Paul is clear on this point.

Christ has made the pleroma available to all men in his chosen and redeemed community here on earth. He writes: "All things [God] made subject under [Christ's] feet, and him he gave as head over the Church, which indeed is his body, the pleroma of him who fills all with all" (Eph 1:23).

The Church then is the pleroma of Christ. Some writers, especially of the past, have understood this Pauline expression as referring to the Church completing the work of Christ. It is true that the Church is the divine instrument through which redemption is applied and extended to the world of men, and hence she may be said to complete the work of the Savior. But St. Paul does not refer to this activity of the Church when he speaks of her pleroma. For him the Church is the pleroma of Christ because she is filled with the same divine fullness of life and power with which Christ himself is filled. Since the pleroma is in the Church, St. Paul is able to hope and wish that all Christians "may be filled unto all the pleroma of God" (Eph 3:19) and that together he and they may attain "to the mature measure of the pleroma of Christ" (Eph 4:13).

We have here a doctrine on the Church's holiness in God which is quite different from the divine engagement with Israel under the Old Law. It is in fact the fulfillment of the latter. The Church containing the fullness of Christ cannot sin. She is forever the faithful Spouse of the Lord. Infidelity cannot obscure her relationship to Christ. All the strong statements on the indefectibility of the Catholic Church have their theological justification in Paul's teaching on the pleroma. The Church is conscious, in faith, of the divine life which is accessible in her to all who seek it and which remains untouched by the faithlessness of her own members.

This is not all, however, that Scripture tells us about the Church. While we learn that the Church of Christ is holy, we are also told in the same Word of God that she is made up of sinners. The Acts of the Apostles and the epistles of St. Paul are full of incidents of varying degrees of importance revealing the power which sin still holds over the members of the Church. We read of envy and jealousy, of parties and party spirit, of laziness and sensuality, of avarice and lying. There were false teachers in the Church spreading doctrines against the gospel, and there were false brethren trying to undo the work of the apostles. It is obvious from the history of the apostolic community that despite the holiness which is claimed for the Church, sin continued to assail her members. Even in the days of her first fervor the Church knew herself to be a holy community made up of sinners.

Sin is not accidental in the Church. It belongs to her condition here on earth to be constantly wrestling with sin, to seek divine pardon for it, and to overcome it by penitence and love. The perfect prayer Christ gave to his people, summing up the situation of the Christian before his heavenly Father, reveals this point very forcefully: "Forgive us our trespasses as we forgive those who trespass against us" is to be the daily petition of Christians, of all Christians. As all of us need our daily bread and ask God for it in the same prayer, so all of us must admit daily before God and to one another that we are sinners. Sin in the Church therefore is nothing occasional which this or that member has the misfortune to commit in unguarded moments; sin is an essential element of the situation in which the Church of Christ finds herself here on earth, and this thanks to every one of her members.

We are sometimes tempted to overlook this fact. Defending as we must the power of grace to transform the heart and the holiness bestowed by divine justification, we are sometimes led to belittle the reality of sin and pretend that it does not belong essentially to our situation in the Church. And yet we are daily taught by the Church's liturgy that we are sinners. In every Mass people, priests, bishop, and pope confess before the whole community and indeed before the whole court of heaven that they have sinned through their fault, through their fault, through their most grievous fault. In the more popular prayers of recent centuries which the Church has recommended and adopted, we daily confess that we are sinners. "Pray for us sinners, now and at the hour of our death" we plead in the Hail Mary. Did the saints on earth have to say these prayers? Yes, even and especially the saints made these public confessions, for none knew as well as they how far they and all men are wounded by sin and constantly in need of God's mercy. Holiness on this earth does not only consist in being like Christ, but also, simultaneously, in recognizing how we are not like Christ, in repenting, asking for mercy, and being redeemed all over again every single day. The Church is holy, but she is the Church of sinners.

Both of these convictions are part of our faith. They are revealed to us in the Scriptures and announced in the Church's liturgy. Both convictions have been defended by the teaching Church. Against the sects accusing the Church of being a house of evil, the magisterium had to proclaim her holiness, and against the sects wishing to restrict the Church to the pure, the same magisterium had to declare the community of the faithful to be a community for sinners. Even though both propositions belong to our faith, they are not easily harmonized. It is in fact the task of the theologians to look more deeply into the holiness of the Church and the sinfulness of her members in order to integrate the two apparently contradictory principles in a coherent doctrine in keeping with Scripture, Catholic tradition, and the experience of faith.

How can we proclaim the Church as the source of holiness in the world and at the same time take seriously our sins, our own and those of the whole community? This is not a theoretical question. On it will depend our understanding of the trials and burdens to which the Church is subject on this earth. On it will depend our attitude to history.

In much of Catholic literature we find, until recently, a tend-

ency to belittle the seriousness of our own faults. We tended
to present them as purely personal shortcomings which did not
affect the life of the whole community. In order to defend the
Church's holiness many well-meaning authors were tempted to
embellish the past, to cover up the truth, and to explain away
the faults of bishops, popes, and Catholic leaders in general.
These attempts are rather typical of the apologetical approach
which has characterized Catholic literature for many centuries.
There was a widespread fear that perfect frankness in regard
to the crimes, omissions, errors, and false policies of our Catholic past would be a scandal to believers and unbelievers alike,
and that it was in the interest of God and his Church to be silent
about our shortcomings and to speak only of what was edifying.

Such an attitude is based on an inadequate understanding of
Scripture. In our modern age, moreover, it has become quite
impractical. It achieves the opposite of what it intends. Today
we feel that such an approach would be insincere and hypocritical. We believe that the sins of the past are less of an obstacle
to unbelievers and a smaller scandal to the faithful than the
smallness of Catholics who think they must tamper with history
to defend God's economy of salvation.

Charles Journet, one of the great theologians of our century,
has proposed and elaborated a magnificent doctrine of the
Church's holiness which permits us—no, inspires us—to confess
the faults of Catholics with readiness and repentance. According to Journet the Church is holy because she is Christ's. In her
we find the new life. Through her gospel, her sacraments, her
orders, her common worship, through the multiple expressions
of her life of charity, we are reborn in Christ and led on the
way of holiness. We belong to her, but—according to Journet—
our sins do not. Our sins are inspired by forces outside the
Church, they are heterogeneous to her life, they exist in spite of
our membership in her. According to this doctrine, we belong
to the Church only by what she has produced in us; our sin

remains outside. The Church is holy and unblemished, "without spot or wrinkle," the Church of sinners, yes, but without sin.

In this elevated theology the borders of the Church pass right through the human heart. The sinful member belongs to the Church by his baptismal character and by whatever else she has produced in him; but not all of him belongs to her. The frontiers of the Church cut right through a man and exclude from her whatever is sinful in his life. To grow in holiness, in the light of this theology, means to enter more deeply into the Church, to let oneself be more profoundly formed by the Church, in other words, to become more Catholic. To sin, in this theology, means to become more divided, to align oneself with unredeemed humanity, to seek inspiration in the area of darkness which is foreign to the Church of Christ.

This grand theology has the simplicity of the gospel and the greatness of vision characteristic of patristic Christianity. It solves in a radical way the apologetical problem of "saving" the holiness of the Church. Since sin does not touch the Church, even though the sinner belongs to her, there is no need whatever to cover up the faults and sins of Catholics. The holiness of the Church is always visible in the grace-inspired lives of Christians; and it is in no way sullied by the sins of Christians, however high their position in the Christian community. To the extent that a man sins, he cuts himself off from the Church and lives a life apart from her. Sinners cannot soil the Church; they can only soil themselves. This is a theology which takes seriously the Pauline doctrine that the Church is the pleroma of Christ.

For many reasons, however, I believe that this theory is not the last word of ecclesiology on the matter. First, by absolving the Church without trial, the responsibility of a community for what happens through its members is not sufficiently appreciated. Secondly, the Church which is free of all sin is not an historical community, but an abstraction. If Charles Journet were right, it would be impossible to write a history of the Church, since not all of this history belonged to her. The greatest objection, however, against a Church untainted by sin, and hence not liable for the faults of its members, is that it does not agree with the Scriptures. The principal witness in this matter is the divine message addressed to the seven Churches in the second and third chapters of the Apocalypse.

The seven letters dictated by the Spirit, Christ's Spirit, are addressed to the "angels" of the Churches, which probably means to their bishops. As we read the letters, however, it becomes clear that through the bishop the entire community is addressed and every single Christian in it. "He who has an ear, let him hear what the Spirit says to the Churches: To him who overcomes, I will give the hidden manna, and I will give him a white pebble, and upon the pebble a new name written, which no one knows except him who receives it" (2:17). The divine message recognizes to the full the personal responsibility of each single Christian. Even when he is surrounded by evil influences, by bad example in the Church or insidious doctrines of false prophets, it is up to him personally to assert his freedom in faith, to remain true to his baptism, and, if need be, to resist the trend of the community. The Spirit threatens with death the members of the Church at Thyatira who let themselves be influenced by a certain evil woman; but to those who remain faithful and reject her teachings he promises relief from their burdens and ultimate victory. "To him who overcomes, and who keeps my works unto the end, I will give authority over the nations" (2:26). In these passages the entire community is addressed, but each member must choose for himself. Each one is responsible only for himself.

But there are other passages also. We read that the Churches are addressed as communities with a common responsibility. As a group they receive praise and blame. To the Church at Ephesus these words are written: "I know thy works and thy labours. . . . Thou hast patience and hast endured for my name, and hast not grown weary. But I have this against thee, that thou hast lost thy first love. Remember therefore whence thou hast fallen, and repent and do the former works; or else I will come to thee, and will move thy lamp-stand out of its place, unless thou repentest" (2:2–6). The lamp-stand, we are told, is the particular Church itself. Unless the community repents and renews its life of faith and holiness, it shall be chastised, shaken, and possibly even wiped out. Such threats are no exceptions. To the Church at Sardis it is written: "I do not find thy works complete before my God. Remember therefore what thou hast received and heard, and observe it and repent. Therefore, if thou wilt not watch, I will come upon thee as a thief, and thou shalt not know at what hour I shall come upon thee" (3:2–3). To the Church at Laodicea these words are addressed: "I know thy works; thou art neither cold nor hot. . . . Thou art lukewarm, neither cold nor hot, and I am about to vomit thee out of my mouth" (3:15–16). Sin may be a personal decision of the heart, and hence, in a strict sense, only persons and not communities can commit it; but here we learn that Christians together are responsible for their community; together they must repent, together they shall be chastised.

The reader is at once reminded of the divine threats to Israel found in the Old Testament. Many of the prophetic themes recur. To the Church at Pergamum it is written: "I have a few things against thee, because thou hast there some who hold the teaching of Balaam, who taught Balak to cast a stumbling-block before the children of Israel, that they might eat and commit fornication" (2:14). According to a popular Jewish interpretation of the events recorded in Numbers 25:1 and 31:16, Balaam counseled the women of the Moabites, through Balak, to surrender themselves to the men of Israel on the condition that these worship the idols of Moab and eat of their sacrifices. There must have been a group of false teachers in the Church of Pergamum who tried to mislead the faithful by means of evil women.

The Christian community is here regarded as vulnerable as was Israel. Even the prophetic theme of "the holy remnant" is struck: the many shall be abandoned and only the few shall be saved. After the Church at Sardis is threatened with divine visitation, "I will come upon thee as a thief," the Spirit adds immediately: "But thou hast a few persons at Sardis who have not defiled their garments, and they shall walk with me in white" (3:4). From the many references to the Old Testament contained in the letters to the Churches, it appears that God's way of governing the people of Israel still finds application, despite the age of fulfillment, in his government of Christian communities. Following the old literary personalizations of Israel (or Jerusalem), the Church at Laodicea is compared to a woman disgracefully uncovered and shortsighted in her folly. The Lord offers her gold that she may buy white clothes for herself to hide the shame of her nakedness and purchase eye salve to be able to see again. And the divine voice continues, reminding the Church at Laodicea of God's demanding love of ancient Israel: "Those whom I love, I rebuke and chastise" (3:19).

From these seven letters to the Churches we are able to draw a number of significant conclusions. The words which God had once addressed to Israel through the prophet Amos, as a key to the understanding of their own history, may still be applied to the Church: "You only have I known of all the families of the earth; therefore I will visit upon you all your iniquities" (3:2). When the Spirit of God repeats to the Church at Laodicea the message he so frequently had announced to the people of Israel, "Those whom I love, I rebuke and chastise," he revealed to them that the tribulations which shall befall the community are not necessarily a shadow of the cross on which Christ died and which all who imitate him must carry, but they may be divine chastisements for the lack of fidelity and the waning of love. Scripture tells us in no uncertain terms that if the Church in a particular area is hit by persecutions, schisms, or any other calamity this may be because she is called to share in the suffering of the Lord, but it may also be because she has not lived up to what the Lord expected from her. We, the Christian community in this world, must suffer, not only because we are holy, but also because we are unholy. This is a significant key for the understanding of the Church's history.

In the first chapters of the Apocalypse the local Churches are regarded as purchased and possessed by Jesus Christ their Lord. As King, Redeemer, and Judge, he stands in their midst holding seven stars in his right hand, and we are told that these stars signify the angels (bishops) of the local Churches (cf. 1:12, 16, 20). At the same time the Churches are not exclusively regarded as indefectible instruments in the hands of Christ. They are also historical communities, composed of human beings and determined by the virtues and vices of their members. In the perspective of the Apocalypse it would be absurd to say that the sins of these Christians did not belong to the Church in which they lived. On the contrary, the local Church is such a closely united family, under the authority of its angel (bishop), that it has a common responsibility for the Christian disloyalty of all its members. Sin is no doubt individual. Sin demands a personal decision, but in the Apocalypse the responsibility for it is shared by the community. In some situations, it is true, only the personally guilty are threatened with punishment; in others, however—and only God knows the reason why—the entire local community, saint and sinner alike, must listen to the divine rebuke and accept the threat of chastisement. We cannot escape the conclusion that for the biblical writer there is a collective responsibility of the Churches for the sins of their members.

In the first chapters of the Apocalypse there is question only of local Churches. We should not hesitate, however, to apply these principles to the Church universal, the one Bride of Christ, since the seven Churches, in the midst of which the divine Lord reveals himself, signify the entire Church on earth. Seven is the number of the divine judgment which redeems and condemns (cf. the seven angels and seven trumpets, Chapter 8), and the seven Churches symbolize the earthly Church in which divine redemption is not yet complete. The heavenly Church is marked by the number twelve. The number of those who are sealed is twelve times twelve thousand, twelve thousand out of every one of the twelve tribes of Israel (cf. Chapter 7).

The Church possesses the fullness of Christ—this we have shown from St. Paul—but as long as she remains on this earth she must forever strive to assimilate this fullness. The Church possesses all holiness, and she must forever acquire all holiness. From the viewpoint of her fullness the Church is the spotless Bride of Christ, but from the viewpoint of her historical development it is still possible to apply to her life the Old Testament dialectic of faithful-unfaithful Israel which we have described above.

This conclusion does not surprise us. In the unity of the divine plan the great biblical themes of the Old Testament must find their application in the New. Whenever we forget that Israel is the stem into which we are grafted and believe that we can afford to forget whence we came, we tend to fall into error and pride, overestimating our earthly condition. In the last chapter, discussing the schism between Juda and Israel, we observed that this biblical theme of the Old Testament could not be applied without qualification to God's people of the New Testament, being one in Christ: there was, nonetheless, a valid application shedding light on our situation in history. We must say the same in regard to the Old Testament theme of Israel as both spouse and adulteress: it has no direct and formal application to God's people under the New Law, but it does have relevance. The theme has in fact been applied to one of the Churches in the Apocalypse.

It is not surprising that we find this viewpoint in the last book of the New Testament, the great eschatological revelation. While the Church is the fulfillment of the promises made to Israel which prepared her and in which she began, the earthly Church herself is only beginning, preparation, and promise in regard to the ultimate fulfillment at the end of time. In the eschatological view of the Apocalypse the Catholic Church, though firmly established in Christ, retains some of the vulnerability of the ancient Israel.

This notion of the Church's holiness does not scandalize us. It is the precise notion which we encounter in the liturgy, the witness to the Church's tradition. There too we find a holy Church, the spouse of Christ, his holy people. We are constantly reminded, however, to distinguish in this people what is holy from what is not yet holy. It is the perpetual task of the Church, as we meet it in the liturgy, to carry on within herself "the discernment of the Christian," as Guardini says, that is, to subject her own life to the judgment of the gospel. The Church is constantly being purified by the Word of God. On the First Sunday of Lent we begin the collect with the words: "O God, who doest purify thy Church by the yearly observance of Lent. . . ." On the Fifteenth Sunday after Pentecost we pray: *Ecclesiam tuam, Domine miseratio continuata mundet* (Let thy uninterrupted mercy cleanse thy Church, O Lord). The Church which possesses the fullness of Christ must nevertheless continually be forgiven and renewed.

Apart from the prayers of the liturgy which specifically allude to the purification of the Church, the entire liturgy, looked upon as celebration of a mystery, draws the Church into the redeeming and renewing grace of her Savior. Certainly, Christ completed the work of redemption when he victoriously died on the cross. The event by which he acquired for himself a holy Church without spot or wrinkle lies in the past. St. Paul writes in Ephesians: "Christ loved the Church, and delivered himself up for her, that he might sanctify her" (5:25). But in the "today" of the liturgy, this past event is constantly present and applied to the Church now. The Church is sanctified every time Christ draws her into his death and resurrection. Hence St. Paul continues the above quotation by adding: "that he might sanctify her, cleansing her in the bath of water by means of the word." Through sacrament and the Word of God the sanctification wrought in the past achieves its effects in the present. As the Church passes through Lent, Passiontide, and Easter, she remembers and almost identifies herself with the ancient Israel yet unredeemed; she repents of her sins, she accuses herself of infidelity at the foot of the cross in order to rise again, to be redeemed all over again, through the Lord's triumph at the Easter Vigil. The *haec nox est* announces that the past breaks forth in the present: "This is the night which purged away the blackness of sin by the light of the fiery pillar. This is the night which at this hour (*hodie*) throughout the world restores to grace and yokes to holiness those who believe in Christ, detaching them from wordly vice and all the murk of sin!" It is in this holy liturgy, combining Word and sacrament, that the Church possesses all that Christ has done for mankind. Yet she must constantly apply this fullness to her own life. She must let what is holy in her because from above, transform what is unholy in her because from below. Through her gospel, her sacraments, and her hierarchical orders the Church shares in the victory of the risen Christ, and it is because of this that she discovers the inadequacy of her historical situation and the constant need of being renewed. According to the Catholic liturgy, the Church's holiness consists above all in her confident penitence.

That the Church herself, though gifted with Christ's fullness, is in constant need of *metanoia* is not usually found in Catholic writers of modern times. Nor do the official statements of bishops and popes make many allusions to the collective responsibility of the Catholic community for the sins of all. Official declarations rarely admit that we, the Catholic community, have sinned and thus are at least partially responsible for the ills that befall the Church, be they schisms, apostasies or opposition in our own ranks.

Separated Christians often rebuke us for this lack of penitence. They call us a proud Church. The most distinguished among these writers do not call us proud because we claim to be the Holy Church of the gospel, indefectibly built up in Christ; they call us proud because we do not admit (what is not in contradiction with this claim) our own shortcomings, our own contributions to the division of Christendom and the dechristianization of modern society. The real reason, however, why the official documents are reluctant to admit our common guilt is not pride; it is, rather, the abuse to which such declarations were exposed after the Reformation. Father Congar has shown in several of his books that the penitent statements of Pope Adrian VI and similar declarations of Cardinal Pole and other ecclesiastics were not received in the spirit of charity but were employed as weapons against the Church by Luther himself and other Protestant authors. While the patristic age and the Middle Ages spoke with great openness about the *metanoia* of the whole Church, the constant need for renewal and reform, post-Reformation Catholicism has usually avoided such confessions for fear of Protestant hostility. The very word "reform" was no longer used by Catholic writers in regard to the Church! In our own day, however, when the ecumenical movement has affected Christians whether Catholic or dissident, it is to be hoped that the official statements of the Church may return to the biblical and liturgical way of confessing our own involvement in the divisions of the past and the miseries of the present. A public admission of our guilt and the ready acknowledgment of our need for *metanoia* as a group give more powerful witness to the holiness of the Church than do the eager attempts to whitewash the past and to shirk our responsibility for history.

As a matter of fact, humble admissions of the faults of our own community are found in papal and episcopal statements of recent years. Referring to the coming Ecumenical Council, Pope John declared in words which have since become famous: "We do not wish to put anyone in history on trial; we shall not seek to establish who was right and who was wrong. Responsibility is divided. We only want to say: let us come together, let us make an end of our divisions."* The same sentiment was expressed by Cardinal Leger, Archbishop of Montreal, in a sermon on Christian unity delivered on January 7, 1962: "The scandalous picture of separated and mutually exclusive communities is the result of a collective sin of Christians. Let no one think that he can point his finger at certain persons or Churches who bear the total responsibility for our present state of dividedness. 'Let him who is without sin cast the first stone' (John 8:3). All Christians must become aware of their common infidelity to the will of Christ, not to accuse one another, but to implore, with one heart, God's collective pardon for their common guilt."

In exactly the same vein, Archbishop Shehan of Baltimore announced a day of prayer for Christian unity: "On the following day should be offered the Mass for the Pardon of Sins. Here the purpose will be to beg God's forgiveness and undoing of the sins which we Catholics have committed against Christian unity, both in our own times and in the past, both in our archdiocese and throughout the world."** The confession of sin and the prayer for pardon and renewal, for the entire Catholic community, are again becoming part of the Church's official utterances.

We must return to our original question. Despite the tremendous difference between the Old Dispensation and the New, the setbacks and disasters in the history of the Church are not only the marks of her similitude to Christ crucified but also, at other times, a divine chastisement for not living up to what is highest in her.

* *Herder-Korrespondenz*, 13 (1959/60), 274.
** *The Catholic Messenger* (Davenport, Iowa), January 11, 1962.

Thus far we have dealt with the certain ground of Scripture and its traditional understanding in the Church. But we must go on asking questions, even if the reply will lie in the free area of theological speculation. Why does God permit that his holy Church be visited by schisms and heresies? What is the meaning of our divisions? Do the schisms contain a message from God addressed to us? And if the divisions are sent to us as chastisement, for what faults are we being punished and what shortcomings must we correct in ourselves? These are not only legitimate questions but necessary ones, founded on the biblical and Catholic conviction that God is the Lord of history and that he reveals his holy will through the course of events.

Johann Moehler, the great German theologian of the last century, threw some light on this question by his original theology of unity and heresy in the Church. According to Moehler's *Einheit in der Kirche* (a book which unfortunately has never been translated into English), the Catholic Church is a community created by a new life, a life which the Holy Ghost continually imparts to those who believe. For Moehler, Christianity is, above all, life: it is life before it is a doctrine, it is life before it is a sacramental gift or a society containing it. Moehler explains what life is in terms of the romantic philosophy for which he had great admiration. Life is reality seen in its constant growth and development and unfolding. Life is in motion precisely because it contains within itself tensions and opposites which it constantly reconciles. Life gives birth to new life because it must forever overcome and synthesize the contrasts within itself. Considering the Church primarily as a life communicated by the Holy Ghost, Moehler understands the Catholic Church as an organic unity of vital tensions constantly bringing forth new life. According to Moehler, opposing trends within the Church, far from being marks of her weakness, are really signs of her untiring vitality, since such opposition generates new life, reconciling the contrasts in a higher unity of one and the same charity. Moehler believed that the emphasis on any particular aspect of Christian life should be accomplished by another current emphasizing the complementary truth, so that the reconciliation of the two trends in the one Church produces new life and richer fruits.

Let us consider examples taken from our own age. If there are those who insist above all on the liturgy, there must be others who insist more on the invisible spiritual life of the mystic. If there are those who attach importance to worldly connections, concordats, and political promises favorable to the Church, there should be others who stress that the Church is in the hands of God and that her only protection is faith and holiness. If there are those who in their spirituality lay stress above all on the encounter with God in faith, there must be others who are more attracted to the mystery of our co-operation with God and hence to ascetical practices and a holy desire for merits. The binding force of these contrasting movements is the charity which makes men qualify their spiritualities through cohesion with the whole Church. This is the charity which the Holy Ghost constantly creates and re-creates to advance the organic unity of Christianity.

What happens if a man or a group of Christians weakens in charity and withdraws from the community, excluding itself from the sharing and reconciling which the Holy Ghost produces in the Church? The contrast which had once caused greater vitality in the Church now abruptly turns into a contradiction no longer alive in the Holy Ghost. According to Moehler, heresy does not result from an error in the mind, but from the waning of charity. The heretic is one who, severing the bonds of love with the community, refuses to let his vital possession of Christianity be constantly influenced, modified, and reconciled by the life of the whole Church. And because he excludes himself from the community of the Spirit, the contrasting current he emphasized before within total Christianity suddenly becomes for him a contradiction, a source of error and isolation, irreconcilable with the Church.

Moehler drew his concrete examples from the history of the early centuries. He did not apply his theological interpretation of heresy to the Protestant Christians who surrounded him, but the reader feels that he had them in mind also. We may safely apply Moehler's observations to them, without thereby committing ourselves completely to his theology. It is possible to emphasize justification by faith within the Church and to make it the central mystery of one's spiritual life; but, as soon as one withdraws and no longer sees this one mystery in vital connection with the others, this trend becomes one-sided, leads to exaggerations, neglects sacramental life, and comes into conflict with the totality of the Christian life. It is possible for Christians within the Church to emphasize the sovereignty of God in their lives and make it their central concern from which all other aspects of the Christian life receive their meaning. But as soon as a man withdraws from the total community and refuses to let his vision of the gospel be constantly carried forward by the reconciling powers of the Holy Ghost, he will belittle the freedom to which man is called by grace, leave orthodoxy, and what was before a contrasting tendency becomes a contradiction in conflict with the life of the Church.

Moehler firmly believed, and in this he was a truly ecumenical thinker, that Christian groups who have lived in contradiction to the Church should, upon returning to her, preserve a proportionate contrast within the unity of fellowship. In other words, when dissident Christians desire to be reconciled with the Church, they should not be made to conform in spirituality and theological outlook to the Catholicism they meet in the Church; rather should they offer their contradictory vision of the gospel to be healed and purified in the Church so that it becomes a contrasting tendency, the source of new vitality for all members of the Church.

We venture to propose that schisms and heresies have often been reactions to certain faults in the Church. A tendency which might have remained a healthy contrast is exaggerated and deformed, because a blameworthy situation in the Church provoked men of little charity. Heresy often is a truth pulled out of its context, an insight into the gospel detached from the whole of the gospel. For example, seeing an overemphasis on visible splendor in the Church, spiritual men who might have lived their contrasting tendency within the Church are so incensed that they revolt against the unity of the Christian community. Seeing an exaggerated stress on works of piety and merit seeking, more austere Christians, loving the mystery of justification by faith, which their more eager brethren accept only implicitly, protest, withdraw, and carry to extreme conclusions a doctrine which they held before within the balance of total Christianity. This does not excuse the men who thus leave the unity God has created; but it partially explains why schisms occurred, and it puts part of the blame, theologically the lesser blame, on the shortcomings in the Church which provoked them.

Our interests here are not historical or psychological speculations. We want to discover what God teaches us through schisms. As we look at the divided state of Christianity, in particular at our Protestant brethren, we must ask: What is the divine message addressed to us through them? We are not asking what the divine message is to *them:* this is for them to discover. We are concerned only with God's word *to ourselves:* and this is a call to repentance. The Protestant revolt, tragically sinful though it was, points to shortcomings within the Church. By looking at them we can detect where we were unfaithful, and where we still may be unfaithful, to the perfect balance of Catholic truth and Catholic life. The divided state of Christianity constantly urges us to examine our conscience. Is the impatient and unjustified rejection of all ecclesiastical jurisdiction by Protestants a sign that we had become, or still are, too legalistic in our approach to the gospel? Is their strong and unjustified annoyance with creeds and definitions a sign that we had become, or still are, too formalistic in our faith? Is their unreasonable emphasis on individual freedom a sign that we did not appreciate, and perhaps do not now fully enjoy, the freedom which is Christ's gift to the Church? At this point the question of *their* sin is not important. However great it may be, we must ask what God means by chastising *us* with their separation. The divisions of Christianity oblige us to a constant examination of conscience. Have we been faithful to all the gifts which Christ has made to his Church?

God rules and guides his Church in many ways. We believe that the Holy Ghost has been given to the Church to inspire the people to know the truth and to strive after greater charity. We believe that the Spirit bestows on our hierarchy the gift of infallibility when they determine the true meaning of the gospel, and imparts the charism of leadership as they steer a fervent community along the path of holiness. But this is not the only way in which God guides his Church. When we become unfaithful and neglect an aspect of the gospel message or turn our hearts away from charity, God sends us saints to remind us and prophets to stir us up. The prophets—and many of our saints have been prophets—are men called to announce God's judgment on us. The prophet is an unpopular man, a man who says what none like to hear, who puts his finger on the sore spots of our Christian conscience. The prophet in the Church is not a preacher noisily denouncing immoral life and the sins of the world; he goes much deeper in his analysis of the spiritual situation of the world and discovers that the real ills of our Christian society are not found in sinners, in what are often called immoral men, but precisely in the good and law-abiding members of the Church. It is not deliberate sin and the violation of God's commandments which mar the spiritual climate of God's Church; it is rather the blindness of the good, the lack of openness to what is most needed, the unwillingness to learn from others, the slowness in seeking new solutions for the problems that beset us. Pharisaism in its many forms is always the great enemy of the Christian life. The prophet is called to awaken the good, and hence he is usually disliked, called a radical (which he may be), avoided or not taken seriously, suspected of unorthodoxy or accused of disloyalty. We have had such prophets in our modern times. To mention only the dead: Léon Bloy and Charles Péguy in France, and in a less literary way, Karl Sonnenschein and Max Metzger in Germany. On a more profound level, more intense and more refined at the same time, Cardinal Newman was a prophet for the Church. There must always be freedom in the Church permitting a prophet to offer the testimony of his word, or of his life, to recall the judgment of God on the community and proclaim the demands of the Word of God.

How does God guide his Church if we are deaf to Catholic teaching? What does he do when the Word no longer stirs us, when we refuse to listen to the saints and ignore or suppress the message of the prophets? Since God is faithful, he will interfere to lead his covenanted people to insight, holiness, and fidelity. The Spirit said to the Church: "Those whom I love I will rebuke and chastise" (Apoc 3:19). It seems to me that if the Catholic people will not apply the fullness of the gospel to their time, God permits that the seed of the gospel will take root outside the Church. Others, outside the Church, shall hunger and thirst after the good things which we neglect inside the Church. They shall be our accusers. They shall try to possess what was meant for us, and for them within the Church. Yet, since the seed of the gospel cannot develop rightly and healthily outside the Church, their strivings will be partially deformed. The growth of the gospel guided by the Spirit requires the environment which God has created for it. Outside of the Church the movements seeking the promises of Christ will always be associated with errors making them ambiguous, and will eventually be turned against the Church herself. This is our chastisement, that God rebukes us through our enemies. Then we begin to lament and ask for God's help, but unless we repent and recognize the measure of our own responsibility, he shall not save us from our opponents and restore us to sanctity.

Must we not say that this happened at the Reformation? The longing for gospel simplicity which should have transformed Christians within the Church inspired those who broke away from her; but because they lacked the guidance of the Church, their movement swerved from the gospel, became partially involved in error, and stirred up political forces in opposition to the true Church of Christ. And not only for lack of gospel simplicity did God punish us: the yearning of the Reformers was directed to other aspects of Christianity which had been neglected in the Church of Christ. Since this Church, however, is the unique community of salvation, the realization of this yearning outside the Church was destined to be contaminated with error and evil forces. God permitted the sins of the men in revolt to chastise the community of his eternal choice, the Catholic Church.

A similar observation should be made about other movements where the gospel yearning leaped still further away from the Church into non-Christian territory. Why did God permit that forces of liberalism militate against the Christian gospel? Was it to punish us for our religious persecutions? God had to send us liberalism before we understood that religious liberty and the equality of men before the law are values revealed, at least implicitly, in the gospel of Christ. This does not make liberalism a Christian movement, or minimize the destruction it has wrought in the heart of our culture, but it does explain its powerful appeal to many men of good will and help us to understand its place in God's history of man. We must oppose this liberalism, the denial of the supernatural, this indifference to the really important things in life; but we must do it with a touch of bad conscience, ready to learn at every moment the virtues we had forgotten and for the sake of which God permitted its ascendancy. Unless we repent, God will not save us.

Must not the same thing be said about the social revolution of the last century? If the Catholic people, and more important still, if Catholic teachers, had always understood the need of social reform and the theological link between gospel holiness and social justice, God might not have permitted the rise of Communism. The same law is observable here. Since the seed of the gospel cannot develop healthily outside the Church, a movement inspired by an authentic concern for the common good was corrupted, at the very start, by materialism and grave errors regarding human nature. Still, God speaks to us through the Communist movement. We must oppose its ideology, must resist atheism and the materialism which through political tyranny is making its way into the hearts of so many people. But since the Communist movement reminds us of what we had forgotten, we shall fight it in a spirit of repentance. I am suspicious of any group opposing Communism which is not, first of all, concerned with social reform! To speak disparagingly of the welfare state is the blindest way to oppose the Communists. The only valid way to fight Communism, according to the above principles, is to foster an increasing socialization, as Pope John XXIII does in his encyclical *Mater et Magistra.* Only when we listen to the divine lessons in history will God vindicate his people.

5

APOLOGETICS AND ECUMENISM
COMPARED

SINCE MANY PEOPLE have the impression that ecumenism is a new form of friendliness and a rather idealistic approach to the grave problem of Christian divisions, I wish to show that, quite to the contrary, ecumenism is a realistic undertaking marked by a rigorous theological method. To bring to light the true character and the startling newness of ecumenism, I wish to compare it to the apologetical approach which has characterized our theological writing for many centuries.

In modern English to be apologetic about something means regretfully to admit a fault and to offer excuses for it, and hence it sounds strange to us that there should be a whole field of Christian study called apologetics. The original meaning of "to apologize," however, is to speak up in defense, and it is in this sense that we understand the term apologetics. It is a defense of the faith.

The Church has always been in need of defending her faith in divine revelation. The reason for this is quite simple. The steps which God took to redeem mankind were *mirabilia*, wonderful works, amazing, startling, wholly from above. They happened, not according to the laws of nature, but according to the sovereign will of the Lord who intervened in history. The saving acts of the eternal God were not in continuity with the world's history, they were not determined by the human situation which preceded them; they were wholly gratuitous and unsolicited. Mercy has been shown to us because God is merciful, and for no other reason. From this it follows that the divine revelation which is recorded in the Scriptures comes to us somewhat as a shock; our reason, our common sense, are baffled and immediately seek arguments that such events cannot be true. When we compare these events with the ordinary course of human history, we discover no parallels for them, and hence we are tempted to find them not only hard to accept but almost incredible. The supernatural by its very nature poses a problem to our reason and demands to be defended before men.

The defense of the faith necessarily belongs to biblical religion. We must examine and vindicate the signs God has given us as guarantee and testimony of his self-revelation. The apostles practiced this kind of apologetics. They proposed argument after argument that the coming of Jesus, his suffering, death, and resurrection were the events redeeming the entire world. They cited the prophecies of the Old Testament which were fulfilled in Christ, they announced the divine power accompanying Jesus in his miracles, and they recounted again and again the appearances of the risen Lord. We can discover this apologetical concern in the very text of the gospel. The speeches of Jesus and the events of his victory were often arranged in the written record in such a way that they served as a powerful defense against unbelievers and the enemies of the gospel.

We discover the same apologetical concern in the Acts, the inspired account of the early Christian communities. To manifest that the Church was truly the messianic community filled with the Spirit, Luke stressed the unity among Christians more than their disagreements, and the common solutions they found for their problems more than the quarrels which preceded them. All the New Testament writers were deeply concerned with defending the gospel, fully aware that such a defense is necessary and will always be necessary.

Apologetics is necessary not only for the sake of unbelievers who attack the foundations of faith, but also for the sake of believing Christians who seek a deeper understanding of divine revelation and its relationship to human knowledge. Being human, we are destined to be seekers, and since the grace of Christ makes our humanity more true, the spiritual quest for greater insight must continue within the faith we have received. We remain inquisitive. We are led to inquire about the foundations of the biblical faith, raise difficulties, and bring to light apparent contradictions which an earlier generation had not discovered. The human mind cannot leave the mysteries God has revealed unrelated to daily experience, science, and philosophy. Believing in God, we search truth more avidly. Can the new understanding which God has revealed in the Scriptures be in radical contradiction to human knowledge? Or can we who believe discover a certain underlying harmony, or at least an analogy, between the truths of God and the insights of men? Since God Almighty is both author of revelation and the creator of man, there can ultimately be no contradiction between what we can learn from the universe created by God and from the Scriptures he inspired. It is again the work of apologetics to investigate these areas, to defend the divine mysteries before the believing mind in search for greater understanding.

Apologetics is an integral part of theology. Unfortunately, apologetics sometimes dominates theology. It is possible to read the Scriptures and to explain the doctrine of the Church exclusively in the light of controversy. Instead of searching for theological insight into the revealed mysteries, an apologetically minded theologian will concern himself only with those questions which are denied or questioned by the Church's opponents. Instead of letting himself be impressed by the message of the Fathers, of St. Thomas, or of any other great author in the

Church, the apologetically minded theologian will notice only those sections in these writings which suit him in the defense of the Catholic position. It is, unfortunately, possible to emphasize the defensive function of theology to such an extent that the whole of its field and activity becomes marked by this one-sided approach. This is what happened in much of the theological literature of the Counter Reformation and in the nineteenth century.

We wish to give a few examples of this tendency. Our first example is taken from ecclesiology. It is well known that the Reformers rejected the institution of the Church such as they found it in their century. In writing of the Christian community they emphasized those passages of Scripture which announce the spiritual and invisible aspect of Christ's body, the union in charity, the freedom in Christ, and rejected as unbiblical a Church claiming to be a visible and juridical society. The reaction of Catholic controversialists and of the great part of Catholic theologians was to emphasize precisely the elements that were neglected or rejected by these Protestants. The treatises on the Church written from the Counter Reformation until the quite recent past were all inspired by an apologetical intention.

The visible, hierarchical, and juridical aspects of the Church were stressed; and only those passages of Scripture and the Catholic tradition were studied which justified this one-sided emphasis. The Church was defined purely and simply in terms of its visible elements. The famous definition of Bellarmine speaks of her as "the community of men assembled by the profession of the true Christian faith, by the communion of the same sacraments, and under the government of legitimate pastors." He wrote: "Sufficient is the external profession of faith and the communion of the sacraments—all things that the sense can recognize. The Church is a community of men as visible and palpable as the community of the Roman people, the kingdom of France, or the republic of Venice." In the heat of the Protestant controversy a definition of the Church was adopted which was silent about the mystery of the Church's existence in Christ and of her soul which is the Holy Ghost.

The second example is taken from the role of the Bible in the Church. It is well known that the Protestant Reformers proclaimed that the Bible was the sole source of divine revelation, and that they rejected from Catholic life and doctrine all that in their eyes could not be justified by Holy Scripture. We realize today that the Reformers were actually much more dependent upon Christian tradition than they were aware of. When they accepted the central doctrines of Christianity, the Trinity and the Incarnation, they believed that they relied on Scripture alone; actually however, they received the scriptural testimony in the light and with the terminology of the early Councils. Because of the Protestant cry of Scripture alone, Catholic controversialists and the majority of Catholic theologians after them put special emphasis on the aspect neglected by the Reformers, that is, the Church's tradition. Whatever of Catholic belief and practice could not readily be proved from the Bible was ascribed to the Catholic tradition, and a theory was devised, based on a certain interpretation of the Council of Trent, according to which there are two sources of faith, two independent sources, one the Bible, and the other the Church's tradition. Certain divine truths were contained in the Bible, and others were supposed to be contained simply in tradition.

In the face of Protestant opposition, the Catholic theologians were forever on the lookout to show that the beliefs of the Church of their day were contained in the documents of the past. There was the constant temptation to let biblical texts say more than they were meant to say, and to interpret the testimonies of the liturgy and the writings of the Fathers in the same apologetical way—collecting ammunition for the controversy with Protestants. When no record of certain ecclesiastical positions could be found in ancient documents, theologians, without proof, made appeal to an oral tradition which was supposed to have existed from apostolic times throughout the centuries to the present day.

Perhaps the Catholic writers of the Counter Reformation had no other choice. The Church had not yet meditated sufficiently on the relation between Scripture and tradition. In the patristic age and the Middle Ages, the Church had always regarded her doctrine as biblical, as based on scriptural revelation. This biblical revelation was understood through the help of the Holy Spirit acting in the Church, so that the decisions of the Councils, the testimony of the Fathers, the liturgical practices of the Church, and the verdicts of the Roman bishops were regarded as authentic and divinely assisted commentaries on the Scriptures. Tradition was not an independent source of faith; it was the totality of the Spirit-guided ecclesiastical witness to the meaning of the Word of God. At the Reformation, Catholic theologians were confronted with a delicate problem which they were unable to solve. The theology which they did propose was unfortunately one-sided.

The consequences of this one-sided emphasis on tradition proper to the Counter Reformation can be found in every branch of theology. The Bible was never forgotten, it was not even neglected, but its use was entirely subordinated to the apologetical intention of refuting the Protestant heresies and of giving proofs for the traditional doctrines of the Church. The Bible was not read in continuity with the purpose of understanding the great biblical doctrines; it was, rather, used like an anthology of inspired sentences which served as arguments for the doctrines of the Church. Biblical passages were cited when they were useful in a theological argument. Instead of interpreting them in their proper context, they were usually understood according to what they sounded like in the contemporary setting. Passages of Scripture were often made to mean what was convenient to the theologian.

This is a method we still find in many of the manuals which are in use at our seminaries. In these books we begin by proposing dogmatic theses and then draw up a list of biblical passages to demonstrate their truth. We can well understand the embarrassment of priests brought up on these manuals, when, years after they have left the seminary, they discover that many of the passages which they had learned as proofs for theological theses have, in reality, a meaning which is quite different. Such an experience may well inspire a sense of insecurity, and the result very often is a resentment against modern biblical scholarship.

I wish to give a third example of changes in theology produced by an apologetical overemphasis. This is taken from the area of faith. It is well known that the Protestant Reformers defined the act of faith largely in terms of confidence and hope. Many of their statements seemed to deny that contained in the act of faith was an assent of the mind to truth. For them, to believe that Jesus was the Savior of mankind was not yet faith. Faith was much more than that: it was the consoling realization that Jesus is my personal Savior now. What counted was the surrender to Christ; the creed or the articles of faith were secondary, and, with certain Protestants, even incidental. Against this doctrine, Catholic controversalists emphasized the intellectual aspect of faith. In fact, so greatly was this side of faith stressed that the conversion implicit in faith was not fully appreciated in Catholic theological writing. Traces of this tendency can be found on every level of religious literature. Faith came to be looked upon mainly as acceptance of a doctrine. To believe was defined as an act of the intellect holding as true the teaching of the Church. While the scholastic tradition of the Middle Ages had given considerable emphasis to the engagement of the will in the act of faith, and had defined this act principally as an encounter with the merciful God revealing himself in Christ, the apologetical concern of post-Reformation theology singled out the intellectual or conceptual aspect of faith.

The practical consequences of such a one-sided theology were considerable. If faith is regarded mainly as saying "yes" to the articles of belief taught by the Church, then the important thing about faith is its correctness, and the elements of surrender contained in it are neglected. What would count is that faith acknowledges the entire doctrine of the Church. This theology of faith determined the form of Catholic catechisms throughout many centuries. If faith was simply holding a doctrine as true, the catechism had to spell out in detail and with systematic precision the teaching of the Church. These dry books, giving summaries of articles of faith in a highly intellectualized form, have remained our catechetical heritage for a long time.

Only in fairly recent years, after the fullness of the ancient Catholic notion of faith had been rediscovered by theological writers, have we experienced a change in our catechetical approach. If faith is the response of the entire personality to God speaking to us, a catechism must not address itself exclusively to the human intellect. It must have a wider appeal. It must announce the "good news." It must present the doctrine of the Church as the gospel of salvation. It must elicit from readers an act of faith which makes them cling to divine Truth as a source of eternal life. Catechetical institutes in various countries have worked out catechisms and schoolbooks based on such a kerygmatic approach, and the Catholic hierarchies of several countries have accepted these new catechisms as the official books of religion to be used in schools.

These three examples from the theology of the Church, the attitude toward the Bible and tradition, and the notion of faith illustrate the powerful effect of apologetical trends on Catholic theology after the Reformation. In those days apologetics was accompanied by another form of literature, polemics, the purpose of which was to attack heretical and unchristian theological positions.

In a sense polemical writings belong to the core of Christian literature. Since the gospel was preached into a world situated in

darkness, it was natural that it would find opposition among men
and be in conflict with other religions. From the beginning it
had been the task of the Church to reject and condemn whatever
was incompatible with the gospel of Jesus. The apostles themselves and many Christian writers after them tried to show the
inadequacies of religious systems in opposition to the Church,
either by detecting the error on which they were built or by un-
masking the evil intentions of their powerful advocates.

At the same time the polemical spirit is susceptible to exaggeration. If it becomes too powerful it will mark all areas of religious
literature and all branches of theology. Then almost every word
on religion will contain an attack against heretics. Polemical
writers are not so much concerned with a positive and profound
exposition of Catholic truth; their special interest is to present
the dangerous teachings of others in the worst possible light, to
refute them, to cover them with contempt and derision. Since the
days of the Reformation this polemical spirit has influenced a
great part of Catholic (and Protestant) literature, and even in our
own time we are conscious that we are still largely surrounded
by it. Our sermons, our pamphlets, our popular books are still
full of the old polemical arguments. There are real dangers in
this approach.

The first danger of the polemical approach is that it often
prevents us from understanding the position of our opponent. We
read through his writings to detect the errors, not to comprehend
what he is saying. It is, alas, possible to read an author without
ever listening to him. We are so determined to prove him wrong
that we go over his writings with red pencil in hand like a school-
master marking an essay. Or, what is worse, we simply rely on
secondhand information. Yet if we do not comprehend the teachings of others, how can our arguments against them ever be
effective? Here we touch the weakest point of the polemical approach. Our refutations may sound quite convincing to ourselves
and to members of our own group who are willing to follow us,

but those who understand the position we try to refute will feel that our arguments are not really to the point. The polemical controversialist often fights a straw man of his own making. Unless we study the beliefs of Protestants from their sources and approach them with the sympathy necessary to understand them, our arguments will not only be meaningless to Protestant Christians, but will also persuade them of our lack of objectivity and love.

This leads us to a second danger of the polemical approach: it tempts us to sin against truth and charity. If our sole concern is to refute the position of our opponents, we shall be constantly tempted to use unfair means in doing so. We might misrepresent their views. We might select one set of quotations which would make a rebuttal easy, and be silent about another set of quotations which would make our task more difficult. We might exaggerate, deform the thought of the others a bit; we might dwell on what we believe to be the motives behind the doctrine or even on the sins and failings of their advocates. In all these cases truth and charity would be offended. Or again, in refuting our opponents we might color the truth a little in our favor, we might deny certain embarrassing facts of history or give credence to legends when they are in our favor. The experience of centuries has taught us that polemical writers are tempted to be disagreeable, to insult their opponents, to qualify their views by offensive adjectives, and in general to create a kind of literature that will engender hate and contempt in one group against the members of another. Polemical literature has been the mother of prejudice.

Against this background we want to understand ecumenism. As a theological and literary method, ecumenism is a remedy for the ill effects and dangers we have found in the apologetical and polemical ways of the past. Ecumenism carries on the essential task of apologetics and polemics, while carefully avoiding their dangers.

This kind of ecumenism did not appear all of a sudden. It is the result of the concerted effort of theologians for over a century. The ecumenical approach did not always have the balanced form it has today; it was elaborated with pain and experiments; yet despite the occasional failures, the daring high paths or deceiving blind alleys, the process of discovery has ripened and the fruits have been tested. In Chapter 2 we saw that the papal documents of our time are themselves witnesses of the changing attitude to Protestants, and they suggest a new theological approach. As a theological method and a literary ideal, ecumenism has reached a point of maturity. It may not yet be influential in all countries, it may not have penetrated to all universities and seminaries, it may still have its declared enemies; but judging from the creative theology which is being produced in our day and the trend followed by an ever-growing number of Catholic journals, we must conclude that the ecumenical approach in theology and theological writing is firmly established in our century. The Roman journal *Gregorianum,* which is certainly not known as avant-garde, recently published an article by Father Witte, professor at the Gregorian University, beginning with a paragraph of a single sentence: "The age of polemical apologetics is past, the age of ecumenical theology has begun."

In what way does ecumenism offer a remedy for the unhappy results of the apologetical and polemical literature of the past? Reversing the order of discussion, we shall first consider how the shortcomings of polemics are overcome.

One of the characteristics of ecumenism is the acknowledgment and appreciation of the Christian elements within Protestant communities. We are conscious today that the virtues of faith, hope, and charity are not confined to the visible boundaries of the Catholic Church, and that whenever separated Christians, separated in good faith, cling to the Savior and to what they know of his economy, they are in vital and supernatural communion with him. Baptized Christians are grafted into Christ and become members of his body. They are our brothers, even when separated. Looking upon Protestants with a new sympathy, we have become concerned about understanding their teaching and their way of life in all truth. The ecumenist does not study the doctrines of others simply to refute them; he wants to listen, to penetrate, to grasp the inspiration and the vision of the whole. Willingness to listen is a prerequisite of intelligent dialogue. In the course of his studies the ecumenist will certainly come upon the errors contained in Protestant doctrine. In fact, he will see them in a sharper light, but his first intention is to understand sympathetically the position of the others.

Some people mistrust this approach. They feel that sympathy in listening to heterodox teaching is dangerous. A Catholic author, in a recent essay on the Anglican mind, asserts that "it is of course not necessary to make a profound study of Anglican religion. We have the truth and are the only true Church." But precisely because we have the truth, we may venture to look at other doctrines with fairness and security, and because we are the true Church, we will have a deep concern for dissident Christians, their life, and their theology. Since the Church regards herself as the mother of the faithful, even when they are separated, she feels even more responsible than do they for Christ's gift of Christian unity.*

The ecumenical approach generates a new moral sense, demanding our loyalty to truth even when it hurts us, and our adhesion to charity even when we disagree radically. We are aware of a new ethics in presenting the teachings of others, in telling their history, and in carrying on a theological argument. We avoid easy and unkind generalizations. We try to present the doctrines of others in their best light; even if these others keep on mis-

---

* Even from the viewpoint of effective controversy, the ecumenical approach to Protestant studies is the more fruitful one. Only when we understand the deep intentions of Protestant thought and the underlying unity behind their theological positions, can we begin a conversation or an argument which will be meaningful.

representing our teaching, we shall not retaliate, convinced that the ecumenical spirit shall eventually conquer all Christians. We shall avoid offensive language. We shall learn to word our deep differences in a way that does not insult our opponents nor suggest that they are inspired by bad will. This ecumenical style has nothing whatever to do with compromise. On the contrary, frankness and clarity are essential if we want to arrive at deep insight into the problems of Christian disunity. But we have to learn to express our total disagreement, if need be, while still remaining in charity. This is not always easy (we have so little practice in doing it), but the effort is demanded by the first commandment of our religion, which is love.

We touch here upon an area where the entire Christian community takes part in the ecumenical movement. In teaching children, in preaching in church, in private conversations and personal arguments we still employ a multitude of expressions, and assert a number of ideas, concerning Protestants (and Jews and others) which sin against truth and charity. Unless our attention has been drawn to it, we do not even notice these things; we simply talk like all the others. Occasionally, however, we become conscious of it. If, for instance, a teacher in a Catholic school knows that a little Protestant girl is in her class, she will take care not to say anything that might offend her, and even when she has to explain in what ways Catholics differed from Protestants, she would find a way of doing it without wounding her pupil. But if no Protestant girl is there, how would she express herself? Might she not use words which generate in her pupils contempt and aversion for persons holding heterodox views? The ecumenical self-discipline in speaking about others is of greatest importance for all educators. All Christians are called to charity, and hence all of us must acquire a certain asceticism of the tongue that we learn to remain in charity, even when expressing radical disagreement.

The ecumenical approach, moreover, overcomes the ills of

the excessive apologetical emphasis introduced into theology and religious literature. We have shown above how the apologetical concern of the past centuries has shifted the emphasis in all areas of theology in a certain, definite direction. Our manuals bear the marks of this anti-Protestant trend on every page. Ecumenism is a theological method by which we correct this bias and establish the Catholic tradition in a more perfect balance. Instead of rejecting the various Protestant positions completely and uncritically, we try to distinguish in them the errors and the authentically Christian aspirations. And instead of creating a Catholic theology with an anti-Protestant bias, we try to show first of all that whatever is truly biblical and Christian in Protestant ideals is actually contained in the ancient Catholic tradition, at least implicitly.

This sentence needs explanation. Some readers unacquainted with Protestant writings and the advance of modern Catholic scholarship on Protestantism, may wonder what we mean by the words "authentically Christian" when applied to Protestant teaching. Without entering into a detailed discussion of the genesis of Protestantism, we may safely admit with all historians that the Reformation was a reaction to something within the Church, a revolt against certain abuses and a new emphasis bringing to the foreground neglected elements of the gospel. The errors of the Reformation lay precisely in this, that they were exaggerated expressions of legitimate concerns. The Lutheran doctrine of justification by faith alone, heretical in some, though not in all its formulations, was a reaction to the loss of the biblical notion of faith among the Catholic people, and the Calvinist doctrine of God's utter and incommunicable transcendence was a reaction against tendencies in Catholic theology and ecclesiastical practice which did not take seriously enough the gulf between God and his creatures. Even the sectarian movements which arose in the Middle Ages, the sixteenth century, and in more recent times, have always emphasized the areas in religion which had been neglected by the Churches from which they broke away. If they rejected the liturgy, it was because they experienced a formalism in established Churches. If they refused to kneel down during prayer, it was because experience had taught them to suspect gestures in our relationship to God. If they avoided churches and built their own little chapels, this was in part because they had been hurt by the coldness, want of simplicity, and lack of brotherhood in the larger Churches. Calling movements of secession reactions does not justify them, nor annul the responsibility of those who instigated them, but it does offer an explanation of the particular direction which the movement took and the speed with which it travelled.

The Catholic ecumenical approach is conscious of the legitimate aspirations of Protestants. We have learned to take Protestant accusations seriously. Instead of rejecting them uncritically and attributing them to bigotry or prejudice, we consider it worthwhile carefully to study the more thoughtful objections to the Catholic Church. These remarks may well contain valuable insights. They may bring to light that we have neglected certain elements of the full Catholic tradition or fallen into one of the many temptations which constantly surround organized religion. There are, of course, uneducated and unkind men who accuse the Catholic Church of all kinds of faults which do not exist except in their own imagination, and it is a waste of time to take these utterances of bigotry seriously. But in the writings of great Protestant theologians and ecclesiastical leaders we find such a high quality of criticism and theological objection that they present a true challenge to us, demanding our most careful attention.

The Catholic ecumenist is willing to learn from Protestants. There exists no *a priori* reason nor theological necessity why the criticism of Christian men outside the Church should not be valid, why it could not remind us of elements of our own tradition which we have neglected. When, for instance, Protestants accuse us of having religious worship which is formalistic, un-biblical, and incomprehensible, leaving the people as passive on-lookers, there is no reason why we should not examine this area of Catholic life in a critical way. It is certainly possible that the Word of God is neglected in our Sunday services. In a deep sense the Word of God is always present since our liturgy contains biblical lessons and since the sermon is part of the Sunday celebration; but in the practical order it may well happen that the biblical texts read quickly in Latin are not understood and appreciated by the people and that the brief sermon does not deal with the message of salvation. If we simply reject the Prot-estant accusation, we shall feel no urgency to change our liturgi-cal life; but if we take their criticism seriously, we shall be in-spired to transform our worship so as to manifest more clearly that it contains the Word of God, and through this Word creates a context in which the sacraments shall be more powerful.

Sometimes Catholics are surprised when they hear a priest asserting that we can learn something from Protestants. Are we not the true Church? Do we not possess the fullness of truth? We do; and yet there is much to learn. We shall enter more deeply into this problem in the next chapter. At this point, however, I wish to give a little example which may convince us more easily: we can learn from Protestants to be on time for Sunday Mass! We know only too well that many of our Catholic people do not arrive punctually for Sunday morning Mass. Most of them will be there when the priest comes out into the sanctuary, but a steady stream of men, women, and children will keep on entering the Church during the first part of the Mass. The priest is very conscious of the fact that almost every Sunday the doors open even during his sermon, letting in new latecomers—who perhaps are not even the last ones. This phe-nomenon is completely unknown in Protestant churches. Here is certainly something we can learn.

We may ask why there is such a difference between Catholic

and Protestant punctuality at church services. It seems to me that there are two reasons, and they are interrelated. First of all, in the Catholic Church going to Mass on Sunday is an obligation. It is a law. Whoever is free to, but does not attend holy Mass commits a grave sin. For this reason many people will attend Mass who would not go if it were up to their own inclination. They will go to Mass, yes, they will even try their best to worship God as they should and ask for his blessing, but they are not sufficiently engaged in this Sunday event to get ready and get their family ready in sufficient time. Since Protestants are not obliged to go to their Sunday worship, only those attend the service who really desire to do so and to be present at all of it.

There is perhaps another reason. For Protestants the entire Sunday service is a unity which cannot be broken down into parts. If you want to attend, you must be present for the entire worship. The Catholic Church, on the other hand, was obliged to introduce a number of divisions in the divine service. Since it is an obligation under sin to attend Mass, theologians had to determine when the persons who came late committed this sin. Is it a sin, mortal or venial, if you arrive at the epistle? Is it a sin, mortal or venial, if you arrive after the offertory? What about the person who arrives after consecration and goes to communion? Has he fulfilled his Sunday obligation? A positive legislation always introduces distinctions and clauses, and presents the constant temptation of legalism. To solve this problem Catholic theologians have introduced the important distinction, derived from Aristotle, between the essential part of the Mass and the accidental parts. To miss the essential part of the Mass would be a grave sin, to miss an accidental part would not be one. Hence one may be tempted to think that one part of the Mass is important because essential, and the others are not important because accidental. While I will not deny the necessity of such a distinction, I still believe this distinction helps to explain why so many Catholics are late for their Sunday worship. They do not experience the Mass as a unity, but think of it as made up of parts of which consecration and communion are really the important ones. It is the intention of the liturgical renewal in the Church to lead the faithful to a deeper personal experience of Sunday worship as the important event of the week, which, though made up of diverse liturgical gestures, constitutes a theological and dramatic unity which should not be broken.

After this digression we must return to our theme: the ecumenical approach as a remedy for the shortcomings of apologetical theology. Ecumenism does not only take seriously the Protestant objections; it also searches to understand and appreciate the valid aspirations in and behind Protestantism. It is part of our faith that whatever is truly Christian belongs to the Church of Christ. The ecumenist is convinced therefore that the authentically Christian aspirations of Protestants are fulfilled, or at least may be fulfilled, in the Catholic Church. The sincere appreciation of the true Christian values among Protestants will lead the ecumenist to an attitude which is quite different from that of the apologetically minded theologian. Instead of explaining Catholic doctrine with an eye to refuting Protestantism and emphasizing the very things they criticize in us, the ecumenical approach seeks to attain a greater balance of Catholic truth and show that the Christian values and insights of Protestants really belong to the Catholic Church. This may mean going back to the sources of Catholic teaching: Scripture, the Fathers of the Church, the liturgy, and the ancient Councils. This may mean subjecting to careful analysis some of the theological ideas which we have taken for granted for a number of centuries. This kind of ecumenical dialogue is an enormous stimulus for creative theological thinking.

We want to be sure that the above paragraph is not misunderstood. Someone might think that ecumenism seeks to accommodate Catholic doctrine to suit the theological preference of dissident Christians, or that a comparative study will lead to a progressive assimilation of various Christian creeds, or that ecumenism desires to accentuate the common elements between Catholics and Protestants, thus leading to an eventual compromise in the realm of doctrine and faith. This undoubtedly presents a temptation. This is the method and the dream of some Protestant theologians belonging to the ecumenical movement. But it is not Catholic. It has been condemned many times by the magisterium of the Church, and there is no Catholic ecumenist of note who has ever expressed the slightest inclination in this direction.

The aim of Catholic ecumenical theology is quite different. It desires to uncover the enormous riches of the Catholic tradition in order to show that the true Christian elements found among Protestants exist in the Church, and will find their fulfillment in that Church. The following paragraphs will make this assertion clearer. Having shown above the harmful effect of a one-sided apologetical approach in various theological areas—the Church, the Bible, and faith—we shall now attempt to show how ecumenical method has purified these areas, made them more biblical and more Catholic.

We have mentioned above that the tendency of the Reformers to speak of an invisible Church provoked Catholic theologians to emphasize what was most contrary to this: namely, the hierarchical structure of the Church. Post-Reformation Catholic literature looked upon the Church mainly from this apologetical point of view, stressing its visibility and its social character: many elements of ecclesiology found in ancient and medieval writers were simply set aside. The ecumenical approach changed this completely. A Protestant emphasis on the spiritual in the notion of the Church led ecumenically minded Catholic theologians to investigate and elaborate precisely the spiritual and mysterious character of the Church within the Catholic tradition. They discovered from the writings of the Fathers, the liturgy, and the great medieval authors that there exists a Catholic vision of the

Church which transcends the somewhat narrow picture drawn in the interest of apologetics. These men reaffirmed that the invisible parts of the Church—faith, grace and Holy Spirit—are really what is primary in the Church, and that it is from them that the visible part derives its meaning and dignity. In modern ecclesiology, as developed by a triumphant procession of great theologians, we encounter the Church as an invisible-visible mystery, written into the gospel, summing up all that Christ has done for humanity; and we discover that we falsify this notion of the Church whenever one side of the Church, the visible or the invisible, is emphasized at the expense of the other.

The name which immediately comes to mind in this connection is Johann Adam Moehler, the great German theologian of the last century. The most famous of his books, entitled *Symbolism*, has been translated into English. Moehler is sometimes called the father of ecumenism. He enriched Catholic literature by a number of profound studies on the mystery of the Church. He opened doors which had long been locked, and gave a great impetus to the development of modern ecclesiology.

Moehler's *Symbolism* is a confrontation of Catholic doctrine with the teachings of the various Protestant Churches. Without using the word, it is in intention an ecumenical study. Moehler criticizes the controversialist literature of the past, both Catholic and Protestant. He realizes that Catholic apologists tended to misrepresent Protestant doctrines: their presentation of Protestant doctrine was usually so one-sided that Protestants did not recognize in it their own beliefs. Even when there was no intention of deceiving, Catholic writers would study individual Protestant teachings separated from the total vision of which they were part, and hence failed to understand what the Protestants had really wanted to express in them. Moehler criticizes, moreover, a readiness among Catholics to rely on the opinion and views of certain authors, instead of studying more closely the objective statements of faith of the various Protestant Churches. In his own book, therefore, Moehler tries to present Protestant teachings carefully, shunning all polemics, depending as much as possible on confessional documents, and attempting to discover the underlying unity and coherence of all these doctrines in some basic principles.

From our modern ecumenical viewpoint, Moehler's tone in the *Symbolism* is still quite apologetical. He does not take sufficiently into account the prophetic character of most Protestant declarations; he tends to regard them as metaphysical statements, as elements of a religious system. He is, moreover, too easily prepared to idealize the Church and to close his eyes to some areas of Catholic theology and certain trends within the Church which irritate Protestant sensitivities.

Yet Moehler is an ecumenical theologian. From his letters we know that the greatest spiritual and intellectual experience of his life was an extended visit at Berlin in 1823, where he came in living contact with a dignified and authentic Protestantism. He attended the lectures of Schleiermacher, Marheinecke, Neander, and other Protestant thinkers, and he was deeply impressed by their scientific earnestness, their religious dedication, and their ready acknowledgment of the merits of other Churches—a rare thing in those days. This profound experience impelled Moehler to study more deeply, with objectivity and dedication, the ancient Catholic tradition and to create from the very substance of the Church the Catholic response to the vital thought of his day. Moehler was never satisfied with a simple No. He wrote that if Catholic theologians should attempt to disregard the age in which they lived, the age would have its revenge: it would disregard Catholic theology. For Moehler theology must be *in* and *above* every period of civilization, *in* because it is human and scientific, and *above* because it is divine and evangelical.

In his *Symbolism* Moehler treats the mystery of the Church in a way which has since become classical. Leaving behind the apologetical concerns of the Counter Reformation, Moehler returns to a concept frequently found in the writings of the Fathers: the Church continues and applies to the men of all times the redemptive work which the Savior completed in glory on the cross. The Church therefore deserves to be called the Incarnation perpetuated. As the Son of God had two natures, one human and one divine, so the Church as the continued Incarnation has a human and a divine side; and as in Christ the entire divine activity in the world operates through his human nature, so in the Church also the saving power of his grace is applied to men through the visible mediation of a society. The human, visible elements of the Church are, therefore, divinely chosen signs announcing redemption and the unique means through which this redemption is communicated. Even the visible structure of the Church is mysterious.

This doctrine of the Church is one root, perhaps the principal one, from which modern ecclesiology has drawn its life and inspiration. It has made its way rather slowly through the Catholic world; our manuals of theology, until recently, never quite trusted it; but eventually it entered the teaching of the ecclesiastical magisterium. Leo XIII in his *Satis Cognitum* teaches an identical doctrine, and Cardinal Suhard in *Growth or Decline* makes several specific references to Moehler's *Symbolism* and his doctrine of the Church.

In our own day many Catholic theologians have become aware of the limits of the patristic notion, renewed and clarified by Moehler, of the Church as Incarnation perpetuated. Understood without qualifications, the doctrine could cover with an aura of divinity all forms of church life and could even consecrate as theandric actions our own shortsighted and stubborn decisions. Understood in an unrestricted way, it could make Catholics insensitive to their own shortcomings and unwilling to follow a movement of renewal.

But the more historical and critical understanding of the Church, characteristic of our time, is also due, at least in part, to another ecumenical figure of the last century, Cardinal Newman. In him we see the combination of two kinds of intellectual dispositions, inclinations which are not usually found together: he was an idealist and an historian, a "Platonist" and an "Aristotelian." He had a clear eye for the invisible reality of religion, and yet he could think and speak of religion only in concrete terms. For him the Church was always the spiritual creation of the new covenant, the holy people of the Lord, and at the same time it was a community involved in the circumstances of history and the guilt of its members. With unswerving faith and the whole conviction of his personality, Newman held these two aspects of the Church inseparably joined together. So certain was he that this vision of things was derived from the gospel that, at the cost of great personal sacrifice, he became a member of the Roman Catholic Church in which the divine gift was proclaimed as wedded to a vital continuity in history .

With all Catholics, Newman believed that the Church is both transcendental and historical. Yet with all Catholics, Newman was unable to propose a perfect theology which expressed and completely harmonized these two aspects of Christ's earthly body. He differed from the majority of Catholic writers in that this theological lacuna did not make him insensitive to the Church's historical and transient face. Though he could not find a perfect explanation for it, he did not close his eyes to the involvement of the Church in the political forces of the day, and to her complicity in many a movement which led to moral failure.

The occasion for writing on this subject was an "ecumenical" one. Newman was in dialogue with Anglican theology. To be more precise, toward the end of his life Newman prepared the third edition of his early work, the *Via Media*, in which he had described his understanding of Anglicanism, to which he then belonged, as a middle road between the two extremes of Protestantism and Romanism. Because so much of what he had then said still corresponded to his deep convictions, save the errors in regard to Rome, he wished to publish his essays in a Catholic edition, equipped with a preface placing the views of his Anglican years in the proper light, and supplying the argument against his own grave accusations.

In the preface, then, Newman had to give an account of what he had described as the abuses of the Roman Church. He could not deny the problem, since he himself had raised it so persuasively. Since the integrity of his opponent was his own, his discussion of the Church's contingent situation had all the marks of what we today call ecumenical. It is true that his proposed theology was not perfect, but his honesty and courage made him tackle a problem without precedent.

His theory is difficult to summarize in a paragraph. The great Cardinal believed that the three offices of the Church—the prophetical, the priestly, and the royal—were not easily harmonized in their exercise here on earth. They were truly possessed by the Church, but their correlation was forever unstable. They could never be lost by the Church, but the strong exercise of any one of them brought with it its own proper temptation.

The Church is prophet; but when she holds up the rule of truth as the rigid norm of her piety and practice, she tends to underestimate the motion of the Spirit in men's hearts. The temptation then, Newman writes, is rationalism. Or again, the Church is priest; but when she draws all men into the sacramental worship of the Father and renders real and palpable the world invisible, she might, if this office were emphasized exclusively, do harm to men's sobriety and common sense. The temptation, then, is superstition. Or again, the Church is king; but when she leads her people on the road to sanctity through rules and regulations, and, if need be, through coercion, she might, unless tempered by piety and truth, do violence to the freedom of God's children. The temptation, then, is tyranny. Ideally, the three offices of the Church are exercised in harmony, and one will see to it that the others do not dominate exclusively: worship will temper rationalism, truth will overcome superstition, and piety will soften the ruling hand. But in the actual situation of the Church, this harmony is unstable. Circumstances demand that one office be emphasized more than another, and thus it would seem that the very strength of the Church in this world is often the occasion of her shortcomings.

There are, of course, inadequacies in this answer. But in it we notice a new way of defending the mystery of the Church on earth, a way based not on self-justification, but on humility and faith.

The above pages have been an illustration of the enormous difference between the apologetical and the ecumenical approaches in theology. We have shown that ecumenism has been a creative force in the growth of modern ecclesiology. This brings us to the second example. We mentioned above that the anti-Protestant stress of apologetical theologians tended to minimize the role of the Bible in Catholic life and to emphasize a rather undefined "tradition." Ecumenical theology seeks to establish a greater balance in this area. Ecumenical theologians appreciate the Protestant concern for the Word of God and try to discover its proper place in the Church as well as its inner relationship to tradition.

Against the *sola scriptura* (Scripture alone) of the Reformers, Catholic apologists emphasized the ecclesiastical testimony so much that they came to the new notion of extrabiblical tradition. The Council of Trent was interpreted as if it had proposed a double-source theory of revelation; that is, a theory according to which the divine word of revelation comes to us partly in the Bible and partly through independent ecclesiastical traditions. Relying on these traditions permitted controversialists and theologians to be less concerned about the Scriptures, to be content with categories far removed from the scriptural books, and to avoid the constant confrontation of their theology with the scriptural testimony. We have already mentioned that the Bible was only too often regarded as a reservoir of proof passages, from which theologians picked the suitable ones to buttress their theses.

It is well worth mentioning at this point that, according to several contemporary Catholic theologians and historians, the Council of Trent did not propose such a double-source theory of revelation; according to these writers the Council of Trent agreed with ancient Catholic teaching that divine revelation is both in Scripture *and* tradition, and that these are not two separate sources, but one single source, since the holy tradition of the Church was the light, the divinely guarded light, in which the Scriptures were read and understood. If this is so, the Catholic theologian of whatever school is constantly required to return to Scripture, and to its reflections in the tradition of the Church, in order to deepen his insights, to correct his too human views, and to submit his theology to the entire biblical testimony. If this is so, Catholic theology cannot be a rational system merely built on a set of articles of faith: Even in its most authentic rational speculations, theology will always revert to the Scriptures to test its results and to strive for an ever greater fidelity to the Word of God.

The ecumenical movement in the Catholic Church (long before it was given this name) has always gone hand in hand with the biblical movement. This is not surprising, for the theologians with a new outlook on Protestant-Catholic relations realized the enormous importance of scriptural studies. They knew that communication between Catholics and Protestants was often impossible for the simple reason that the language and ideas used by the two groups had moved too far apart. A return to biblical terms and ideas, however, made a dialogue possible, fruitful, and enriching for both sides. The ecumenically minded theologian, moreover, suffered more than any other from the unbiblical flavor of our manuals and from the neglect of many biblical themes by what was then regarded as traditional theology.

At the same time Catholic biblical scholars have always been sympathetic to the ecumenical movement within the Church and interested in bettering relations with Protestant Christians. Why? Because they often made use of Protestant books on the Bible and were influenced by the great Protestant theologians and their insights into the meaning of Scripture. There is no reason to be ashamed of this. It is simply an established fact. Without Protestant biblical scholarship, the biblical renewal that has taken place in the Catholic Church would have been impossible. This does not mean that our exegetes have blindly followed non-Catholic scholars, or that they have adopted a particularly Protestant outlook in religion. No, the use of Protestant exegesis has always been, and must always be, critical and judicious, for the significant reason that the divine truth in Scripture cannot be discovered by purely scientific and literary means. To understand the meaning of Scripture, faith is required. The Spirit himself, speaking to us most eminently through the teaching voice of the Church, is the unique infallible interpreter of the Word of God. Ultimately the meaning of Scripture can be understood only from within the Church. But this does not mean that Catholics cannot learn a great deal from Protestant scholarship. Today we have our own school of exegetes and biblical research. But the constant contact between Catholic and Protestant scholars makes them friends of the ecumenical movement.

The new emphasis on the Bible, characteristic of our time, is not only noticeable on the level of theology; it is felt throughout the whole life of the Church. There are first of all the many new translations of the Bible into modern languages, and their ever-growing distribution among the people. The liturgical movement, teaching us a new appreciation of the sacred texts employed in public worship, has also brought the Bible closer to the hearts of the faithful. If it is true that Catholic piety and

Catholic religious art are being transformed according to liturgical principles, this means that in the same proportion the influence of the Bible on the daily lives of Christians is growing.

The ecumenical approach in theology, then, has brought a new emphasis on Holy Scripture. If we compare contemporary articles, monographs, or treatises on theology with those written fifty years ago, the evolution of the place of Scripture is amazing. I shall give one significant example.

Let us compare two theological articles on "Faith," one of them written fifty years ago in the *Catholic Encyclopedia,* and the other written recently for a new French encyclopedia called *Catholicisme.* The article in the *Catholic Encyclopedia* contains half a column on Holy Scripture. The first remark is that in the Old Testament faith means steadfastness and is applied both to God and to man. When attributed to God it means God's faithfulness, and when to man it refers to his trust in the divine promise. However, already in the eighth line the author introduces his apologetical concern and asserts that this notion of faith as trust does not exclude belief. Instead of telling us what faith really means in the Scriptures, he goes on explaining what it does not exclude. The author is even more brief on the New Testament. Here too, he begins as apologist, saying that the intellectual assent to a doctrine is included in the notion of faith found in the New Testament. He then cites a few extreme Protestant interpretations on what faith means in the Bible and proceeds to show how these lead to vagueness and subjectivity in religion. This is all the article tells us about the Bible! The next fourteen columns deal with a highly technical theology of faith. Here again, the apologetical concern of the author determines his choice of material and emphasis. He presents a traditional doctrine based mainly on St. Thomas, analyzing faith as act and as virtue, and showing that its subject is the human intellect. He emphasizes especially what the Vatican Council had to say about faith against the fideism and rationalism of its day. But the author leaves out many themes of the immensely rich Thomistic theology on faith. He does not adequately treat of the role of love in faith, he never mentions our justification which is by faith, and he is silent on the vital link with Christ's passion which faith establishes in us. On all of these doctrines St. Thomas is quite emphatic. Faithful to the tradition in which he was brought up, the author does not seek a balanced picture of the Catholic doctrine on faith, but simply presents Catholic teaching with the stress on precisely those elements against which Protestants and other opponents of the Church had objected.

The article "Foi" in the encyclopedia *Catholicisme* is so different in style and content that we wonder how such an evolution could have taken place in only half a century. The article begins with eight columns on the Scriptures. There is, first, a brief outline of how the word "faith" was used throughout the history of Israel, and then follows an analysis of its meaning. While the author shows how faith signified the surrender of the person, or the people, to the living God who acted through them in history, he also explains in proper proportion, without the stress of the apologist, the role of freedom and understanding in the act of faith. Coming to the New Testament, the author traces the notion of faith through the various biblical books, laying stress on the richness and flexibility of this notion in revelation. Faith is not a clear-cut idea, but an attitude of several facets, all dealing with man's radical surrender to God, to the God who acted in history for the sake of a community. Again the author mentions, in proper proportion, the aspect of faith meaning belief in a doctrine.

The article then presents the voice of the magisterium on faith. He singles out three Councils, the second provincial Council of Orange, and the general Councils of Trent and the Vatican, putting their teaching in the proper historical settings. (The first article mentioned above had, characteristically, never referred to the Council of Orange!) The third part of the article in *Catholicisme* deals with the theology of faith, and this from two points of view, faith as conversion to God and faith as belief in a doctrine. Only this very last section deals with the material that was discussed throughout the entire article in the *Catholic Encyclopedia*. The ecumenical and biblical approach chosen by the author of the more recent article cured him of one-sidedness and enlarged his view. He does not avoid Scripture, but makes use of it as much as possible. He does not color the teaching of Scripture, even if at first glance this might appear apologetically embarrassing. The Catholic theologian can approach Scripture fearlessly, precisely because he believes that his Church is the Church of the Lord, and hence cannot be in contradiction with Scripture. The ecumenical approach frees the author from the limiting preoccupation with the theme of his opponents. He becomes large in vision, and treats his subject from all points of view, even from those that are particularly appealing to Protestants.

This example leads us to the third area of theology in which, by way of illustration, we had remarked the shortcomings of the apologetical method. The Protestant tendency to belittle, or even deny, the assent to truth in the act of faith had provoked the contrary emphasis in Catholic writers. For centuries we looked on faith almost exclusively as the intellect's acceptance of a doctrine. The article on faith in the *Catholic Encyclopedia* is a good example of this tendency, taken from the early twentieth century. The ecumenical approach, by passing beyond apologetics, has initiated a considerable change in the theological situation of our day. No contemporary Catholic theologian who is at all up-to-date in theological literature would dream of writing about faith exclusively as an intellectual assent. In our day it is simply taken for granted to speak of faith in a more biblical way as encounter and engagement of the whole man with the self-revealing God, a human act in which the commitment of the mind to truth has its proper place. The article on faith from the contemporary encyclopedia *Catholicisme* is altogether representative of this theology.

On a previous page we have suggested that a more biblical notion of faith has made us aware of the inadequacies of our Catholic catechisms, which address themselves exclusively to the intellect of their readers. We also mentioned that, thanks to a strong catechetical movement in various countries, new catechisms and books on religion have been published—and in large part been adopted by the hierarchy—which present the Church's doctrine as the "good news" of our redemption, as the divine source of wisdom and life.

The above discussion has brought to light the profound difference between apologetical and ecumenical methods in theology. These methods really correspond to two different mentalities; and it is not always easy to pass from one to the other. Since our emotional life is linked to our deep theological convictions, the spontaneous reactions of apologist and ecumenist will often be quite different. If both read the same Protestant book, the apologist will instinctively remark and remember the weak passages, the inadequate proofs, the limited insights, for in his mind the rebuttal is already taking shape. The ecumenist on the other hand, while not insensitive to the weaknesses and errors of the book, will instinctively lay hold of the paragraphs which reveal the deep intention of the author, the central intuition; and before he thinks of arguing against the positions of the book, he will try to understand how the errors and false details could possibly make sense in the mind of an intelligent author. If both the apologist and the ecumenist will, by way of response, write a Catholic exposition on the same theme, the one will spontaneously stress the very points denied by the Protestant, while the other by natural inclination will take care to present the Catholic view in perfect balance, making sure that the true insights of the Protestant author are included, and that his errors are refuted in proper proportion.

As we have seen, there are, of course, situations in the Church where apologetics is required. In this world, the gospel must always defend itself. If malicious slander and prejudice are spread against the Church of Christ, we must defend ourselves. If movements, spiritual or political, threaten the gifts of Christ entrusted to the Church, we must not only defend ourselves, but even attack, in fair and honest polemical writings, the very movements working against us. This however is not the situation of the Catholic Church surrounded by an ecumenical Protestantism. There are certain sectarian groups, certain Protestant societies and periodicals, especially in North America, which are as yet untouched by the ecumenical spirit and the charity which seeks fairness and sympathy for other Christians. There are, alas, certain Christian groups without any tradition of learning who base their beliefs and their dislikes on a most naive reading of the Scriptures and the prejudices which they have inherited from a more superstitious age. Here defense and arguments are necessary.

At the same time, our apologetics will be more intelligent if it is transformed by the ecumenical approach. If we want to defend Catholic doctrine against the objections of these sectarian Christians, we shall do so much better if we learn to speak a language they understand and express our faith in such a way that their Christian insights, however limited they may be, will be saved in it rather than suppressed. Our polemics against other doctrines will be much more effective if we really understand what these others are teaching; otherwise, it may happen that our arguments attack positions which are not really held by anyone.

Except in these exceptional cases, we must unlearn many things that the apologetics of the past has taught us. Ecumenism is something relatively new. We know from experience that the difference between these two ways is so great that intelligent communication between an ecumenically minded and an apologetically minded person is often extremely difficult. If, for instance, an apologetically minded Protestant reads our paragraphs on the changes induced in Catholic theology during the Counter Reformation, he will use this as an argument against the Catholic Church: he will claim that after the Reformation the Catholic Church is in no more direct sense heir of the medieval Church than are the Reformed Churches. I have actually seen this argument used in a polemical book of a Protestant author, and the "proofs" of this unusual assertion were taken precisely from a Catholic ecumenical theologian. Or, to give an example from our own midst, let us consider the humble public confessions made by the general assemblies of the World Council of Churches. Realizing the Christian responsibility for all of humanity, these Protestants felt that much of the unbelief of the modern world and the enmity against the gospel were due to their own failure to convey the wonders of the Christian faith to those who do not yet believe. Thus we read that the ecumenical Christianity assembled at Amsterdam confessed "deep shame and penitence for its failure to manifest Jesus Christ to men as he really is." If this profoundly Christian sentiment is read by an apologetically minded Catholic, he would see in it an admission of defeat and use it in his writings as a proof that now the Protestants themselves recognize that they should never have broken away from the Catholic Church.

Conversation is not only difficult from one Church to another; even within the same Church apologists and ecumenists do not always understand one another. There are many instances where Catholic ecumenical writers present Catholic teaching and Catholic history in a way that appears disloyal and offensive to apologetically minded Catholic readers. This is especially true when it is a question of freely admitting our faults in the past and confessing the inadequacies of some of our theological positions. The ecumenist feels that a humble confession of our own shortcomings is simply a part of Christian honesty and hence must ultimately benefit the Church of Christ, while the apologist feels that such frankness may provide arguments for the enemies of the faith. The standards may vary from country to country, depending on the intellectual atmosphere by which the Church is surrounded, but on the whole, in our day, free admission of faults is a much better defense of the Christian name than are the perpetual attempts at self-justification. Precisely because the Catholic believes that his Church is the unique Church of Jesus Christ, infallible in her dogmatic teaching and in the communication of grace, can he afford to be frank about the failures of his own group.

We must admit that in the past we used to get a good deal of satisfaction from the misfortunes of Protestants, and Protestants enjoyed our own defeats. This *Schadenfreude*, alas, was perfectly mutual. The deep reason why Christians sought to hide their own failures from the gaze of their separated brethren was to keep them from glorying in their own discomforts. Today this has changed. Ecumenically minded Catholics and Protestants regret the waning of Christian faith wherever they see it and rejoice in the triumph of the Holy Ghost wherever it may be. This attitude is not yet universal, but those who have experienced ecumenical fellowship with separated Christians know that it is a reality. If the misfortunes suffered by Protestant Christians no longer gratify us, we will discover the greatness of heart to be honest about our own failures, trusting that the others will be sorrowful with us and not triumph over our weakness. Ecumenism leads to a re-education of our religious sentiment.

It should be clear to the reader that the ecumenical approach we advocate in these pages is quite removed from compromises in matters of Catholic truth, from ambiguity of expressions and the obscuring of dogmatic differences. On the contrary, ecumenical theology is conscious of the deep divergence between the Church's teaching and that of other Christians, and hence it is constantly seeking to remove apparent contradictions to discover the true opposition. Even among the leading Protestant theologians of our day, we find no desire to water down dogmatic Christianity. In Protestant circles of authentic ecumenism the attempt to blur the lines of demarcation is regarded as a betrayal. This willingness to face radical differences makes it possible for Catholics to carry on ecumenical dialogue with such Protestants, and the rules suggested by them for such a dialogue may well be acceptable to us.

The rules for ecumenical dialogue proposed by Dr. Robert McAfee Brown and published simultaneously (February 16, 1960) in the *Commonweal* and the *Christian Century* sum up an attitude with which a Catholic may wholeheartedly agree. These are the rules:

1. Each partner must believe that the other is speaking in good faith.
2. Each partner must have a clear understanding of his own faith.
3. Each partner must strive for a clear understanding of the faith of the other.
4. Each partner must accept responsibility in humility and penitence for what his group has done, or is doing, to foster and perpetuate division.
5. Each partner must forthrightly face the issues which cause separation as well as those which create unity.
6. Each partner must recognize that all that can be done with the dialogue is to offer it up to God.

The last point, it would seem to me, is not strong enough. Much more can be done with the dialogue and its results than to offer them up to God. The dialogue is a spiritual thing and hence a means for self-searching and interior renewal. There is no reason why one should not make the sixth rule read: Each partner must seek to make the dialogue a source of renewal in his own Church.

6

PRESENT ACHIEVEMENTS OF ECUMENISM

CATHOLIC ECUMENISTS are sometimes accused of idealism. They are reminded that the dialogue with Protestants is a waste of time, since no separated group will ever return to the Catholic Church. You have carried on discussions for so long, the critic will say, and there are no tangible results to show for your work. The Catholic ecumenist must ask himself in all seriousness whether his efforts are justified and what precisely he expects from the ecumenical movement.

The aim of the ecumenical movement is the unity of all Christians. It would be quite unrealistic, however, to entertain the expectation that this return to unity will happen in our century. We are far from it. It may even be that in God's inscrutable plan the unity of all Christians is an eschatological event never to be realized until God himself unifies the community of believers at the end of history. Yet it would be wrong to think that the ecumenical movement, inspired by the gospel ideal of unity, does not produce valuable effects on the various Churches prior to its ultimate fulfillment. The ecumenical movement has given to Protestantism a new openness to the voice of tradition and to the fullness of Scripture. The effects of the movement on the Catholic Church have been the creation of a new spirit, a new sense of urgency in regard to unity and renewal, and a universal striving for a more balanced possession of our full Catholic tradition, which will make more evident its substantial conformity with the Scriptures. Without the slightest degree of compromise or vagueness in matters of faith, the ecumenical movement has reduced the distance between Protestants and Catholics, and drawn both groups into a more biblical and liturgical experience of the gifts of Christ. Ecumenism leads all Christians, Catholics included, into the center of the Christian faith and makes the realities of the gospel more vital and meaningful.

In this chapter I wish to illustrate this *rapprochement* between Protestants and Catholics by a few practical examples, and I hope to show the theological depths to which the movement has penetrated.

The first example is taken from the realm of church architecture. In America, but more especially in Europe where the ecumenical movement has been going on for at least one generation, the style of church architecture has undergone a most significant change. While Catholics have a tradition, a brief but strong tradition, of ornate churches, full of altars, statues, niches, exuberant forms, marble pillars, and gilt capitals, the churches built by Catholics in our day have changed. They symbolize above all the simplicity and brotherhood of the community. Churches have become bright and spacious halls with daylight flooding into the sanctuary where the free-standing altar attracts the eyes of all. There is a concentration on essentials. Whatever may distract from the mystery of our redemption is left out: together we stand about the Lord, offering ourselves along with him to the eternal Father. Catholic churches have become houses of worship, not so much for private devotions as for a common liturgy.

At the same time, we find that Protestant church architecture has also undergone a change. Protestants may have a tradition of bare, unattractive, and inartistic buildings; yet in recent years they have discovered the significance of architectural symbolism. Reacting against the individualism of the past, Protestants have begun to build churches full of liturgical feeling, decorated with signs and symbols of the Christian faith, and equipped with a cross and an altar. While in the past their churches were halls in which the Spirit touched the hearts of each believer, they have become temples in which the faithful are united to Christ, the eternal High Priest, offering with him a liturgical worship. A remarkable thing has happened. Catholic church architecture has become more evangelical and Protestant architecture more liturgical, with the final result that the difference between our church buildings and their spiritual symbolisms has become very small. This *rapprochement* is not purely external. It reveals, rather, a theological development on both sides.

Here is another example, this time from the realm of piety, to show that the ecumenical movement produces changes in Catholic life which enrich it tremendously, make it more truly Catholic, and render it more transparent to the eyes of Protestant Christians. In Germany the Catholic bishops publish official diocesan prayer books, containing devotions and hymns to be used by the people in church, and guiding them in their private prayers at home. These books are authentic reflections of Catholic piety. Since the diocesan prayer books are altered and republished about every ten years, it is easy to compare the piety and spirituality of the German people over a given period of time. The change which has taken place over the last fifty years is remakable. The prayer books of 1910 principally contained private devotions for the attendance at Mass and particular devotions to various aspects of Christ's life, his cross, the nails, the shroud, and to the many saints of heaven. These books certainly represent a piety which is truly Catholic; there is nothing whatever dogmatically wrong with them. And yet we find in them a touch of sentimentalism, of baroque exaggeration. They encouraged individualism; they attributed too much importance to incidentals. They did not lead the people into the center of the Church. Moreover, they embodied those aspects of Catholicism which were particularly displeasing to German Protestants.

If we cast a glance at the diocesan prayer books of 1960, we are impressed by the enormous change that has taken place in them. They contain first of all the principal parts of the Church's liturgy. The other prayers and devotions for common and private use, whether they be in honor of the Blessed Trinity, of Christ, of his holy mother or the saints, have a biblical and liturgical flavor throughout. These books represent a piety which is simple, virile, evangelical, and as Christ-centered as the gospel itself. They lead people from the circumference of the Church into the center of Catholic living. They embody the central and biblical elements of Catholicism, the elements which are the most understandable and attractive to German Protestants.

How has this change taken place? Largely through the liturgical movement. The liturgical renewal in Germany has always been the ally of ecumenism. Along with the study of the liturgy, the dialogue with Lutheran Christians has helped Catholics in Germany to discover the one-sidedness of their devotional life and their lack of biblical inspiration. They were led to the insight that all Catholic devotion, even that which we offer to the saints and their relics, must increase our union with Christ the Lord and our share in his mystical body. Thus Catholic piety has become more truly Catholic and at the same time closer to Protestant ideals.

Can similar changes be detected on the North American continent? The situation here is somewhat different. The ecumenical movement is comparatively new among us and has not penetrated large groups of our own Catholic people or the vast body of Protestant Christians. The liturgical movement has worked very hard on this continent, but its influence so far has been rather limited. The majority of our priests and our people do not feel the urgency to alter their ways of prayer. On the whole, they are not unhappy about the distance of the liturgy from the average churchgoing person, nor do they suffer from the comparative incomprehension with which Protestants regard our whole public worship. For this reason we are unable to detect a change of such remarkable proportions as we find in Germany.

A certain change, however, is also visible in the United States and Canada. An ecumenically minded Catholic attending the "Bible Vigils" arranged by the Grail Movement and other groups, becomes convinced that it is possible, on this continent, to renew Catholic spirituality through a closer contact with the Scriptures. He begins to hope that these vigils are tokens of a brighter future in which popular piety will be more deeply determined by God's Word, and the rhythms of prayer and liturgy will echo the simplicity and directness of the inspired Scriptures.

Among the American Churches of the Reformation we observe a constantly growing stress on sacramental life and common worship, and a definite return to orthodoxy in the texts and formulas used in prayer. Here again, it is easy to compare the official rituals of the various Churches over the last few decades. However, instead of giving examples and particular applications, we must pose a deeper question: What does this change represent? Is this only a superficial transformation, a fashion, a fad, or does this evolution correspond to a deepening of the Christian faith? Since no man can look into the heart of another, we must try to gain some insight into the situation by studying the sacramental doctrine taught by the various Christian Churches. Without much effort we can discover that in the last fifty years the whole domain of sacramental theology has undergone a considerable change, among both Catholics and Protestants. We shall try to show in the following pages that it was the ecumenical spirit which opened the door to this evolution and in some cases actually initiated it.

Let us look first at the Catholic side. We have already mentioned that the tendency of sacramental theology after the Reformation was largely determined by anti-Protestant preoccupations. This made itself felt in various ways. Since the Reformers denied that the Christian sacraments were true causes of grace, Catholic controversialists emphasized this very point. They concentrated on the objective efficacy of the sacraments. They proved from Scripture and the tradition of the Church that the sacraments produced their effect *ex opere operato,* independently of faith. Faith was regarded "merely" as a necessary condition for the reception of the sacraments. When the sacraments were studied in this light, the mode of their instrumentality came to be the subject which occupied the interest of theologians. It is true, this subject had already been discussed in the Middle Ages, but the period following the Reformation saw a tremendous expansion of this area of research. If we regard the sacraments mainly as causes, then in addition to their efficacy, it is their validity which interests the theologian most. Under what precise circumstances is this sacrament validly administered? Under what conditions does it produce its full effect? There is room here for endless investigations.

This emphasis on efficacy and validity did not help much to dissipate the grave accusations Protestants made against the whole Catholic sacramental system. Since all that seemed to count was the performance of the rite, Protestants felt that the role of faith in the reception of the sacraments was minimized, or even neglected, in the Church. They accused the Catholic Church of claiming power over grace, of manipulating the divine favor, of trying to handle God, of wishing to mechanize man's relationship with his eternal Savior. These Protestants liked to speak of the materialization of grace which was supposed to have occurred in the Catholic Church. They believed that for the Catholic grace is some thin spiritual substance poured into the soul by God through specially adapted faucets called the sacraments. This was of course a terrible caricature of Catholic belief, but the Catholic's theological preoccupation with instrumentality did not help to enlighten Protestants.

Since throughout these centuries Protestant Christians had denied, in opposition to Catholic tradition, all direct operative power in the sacraments, the apologetically minded Catholic theologian believed he could render no better service to the Church than to defend in strongest terms what had been attacked by heretics. It did not occur to him to work out a sacramental theology which would clarify the positive role of faith in sacramental life and avoid anything that smacked of magic and the mechanical in Catholic doctrine.

A return to a wider theology of the sacraments has taken place only in fairly recent years. The liturgical movement and ecumenism were here, too, among the driving forces. A deeper study of the magnificent theology of St. Thomas also made our notion of the sacraments more truly evangelical. While it is true that many of the themes treated by the theologians of the Baroque period occurred in St. Thomas's writings, they appeared in Thomas as elements of a flexible, living, and ever-widening synthesis of truly evangelical inspiration. For St. Thomas the sacraments are, above all, signs. They are signs announcing our salvation and the redemptive action with which God embraces the recipient of the sacrament. The sacraments are signs of an altogether special kind, for not only do they announce a divine action, but they also produce what they announce. But this power of the sacraments to communicate grace directly does not overshadow their more fundamental character as signs. The sacramental gestures announce the faith to the whole community, and hence from this perspective have an essential connection with the faith of the people. In fact, for St. Thomas the sacraments are closely and inseparably linked to faith. As God communicates himself to men in an undivided fashion through the Word and the sacrament, so men received the gifts of God in an undivided gesture of surrender: faith in the Word and the reception of the sacraments.

The return to St. Thomas, then, led the Catholic theologians of our time to appreciate anew the sign-character of the sacraments. Are these two emphases on sacraments-as-cause and sacraments-as-sign of purely theoretical interest, or are there practical consequences connected with them? It is easy to see that if I regard baptism, for instance, mainly as cause, then all that matters is its validity. It does not make much difference whether the ceremony is performed in a dark corner of the church, seen and understood by few, or whether it is given a place of honor in the church in such a way that the faithful behold the symbols and share in them. If I emphasize the question of validity, I begin to look upon the Church's liturgy as a complex set of rubrics. Priests who are brought up on the notion that sacraments are first of all causes will be mainly concerned in their liturgical exercises with the performance of all the rules and regulations.

If, however, we look upon the sacraments first of all as signs, albeit as very special signs, the principal concern of the priest will be whether the sign has been announced to, and understood by, the people. If sacraments are signs, it does make an enormous difference whether baptism is administered in a corner of the church or in full sight of the faithful. The validity is the same in both cases, but the fullness of meaning which Christ has attached to his sacraments is not reached unless they announce, and announce in power, the wonderful works of God in the community. The liturgy, quite apart from its sacramental value, becomes an authentic way of announcing the death and resurrection of Jesus Christ. The ritual strengthens the faith of all who participate in it, thus preparing them for the high point of the celebration, which is the sacramental encounter with Jesus Christ.

In modern Catholic theology a Christian sacrament is increasingly regarded as a personal encounter with the risen Lord. The sacramental gesture to which we submit announces and renders present to us what the Lord did for his Church. In baptism, it is Christ's death and resurrection which become available to us. The act of receiving these sacraments expresses our faith in Jesus Christ thus acting in his Church, and as we open our souls to him in this surrender of faith, he sovereignly acts in us through the sacred rite instituted by him. The *ex opere operato* character of the sacraments announces the glorious power of the risen Christ over the Church and the hearts of men.

In this connection we must mention another limiting effect of the Counter Reformation on Catholic theology. Since Protestants belittled the role of the sacraments in the Church and concentrated almost exclusively on preaching and the reading of the Bible, Catholic theologians stressed the sacramental means of grace to such an extent that they left undeveloped the role of the Word of God in the Church. It is well known that our "traditional" theology has almost nothing to say about the Word of God. We have mentioned that the Bible was considered mainly as an historical document, from which we could prove the divine claims of the Church and the gospel origin of her doctrines. These theologians did not meditate on what the Bible really was in terms of the divine economy. It is also true, alas, that the traditional theology which has created the manuals in use at our seminaries has nothing to say about the role of preaching in the Church. Because of the anti-Protestant emphasis, we have come to think that the sacraments are strong while the Word is weak, that the sacraments give us grace while the Word gives us only truths. Influenced by this kind of reasoning, many Catholics have come to regard the sacraments of the Church as the only means of grace, forgetting that the Word too is an instrument of divine mercy in this world.

The ecumenical dialogue with Protestant Christians has made Catholic theologians very conscious of this neglect. Returning to the Scriptures, to the Fathers and medieval theologians, they found a mulititude of witnesses to the power of God's Word in the Church. The Word is not only a source of information providing us with the articles of faith; it is at the same time a divine way of acting in the world. God judges and redeems us through the power of his Word. The Bible is a means of grace in the Church, and he who reads it with simple faith opens his heart to the forgiveness of God. *Per evangelica dicta deleantur nostra delicta.* It took the ecumenical spirit and the liberation from the old polemical obsession to rediscover these ancient truths. God's Word is power. This Word of God which creates, redeems, judges, and glorifies, is active in the Church not only through the Scriptures; it is in our midst also through the preaching of the priest in the community. The ecumenical dialogue has led Catholic theologians to elaborate a theology of preaching, showing from ancient witnesses that the annunciation of the gospel in our pulpits makes the word of Christ available to those who listen and believe. Preaching is truly divine, quasi-sacramental activity in the Church. We have discovered again that both the sacrament and the Word are strong in the Church of God.

Since it is our aim in this chapter to outline the actual effects of ecumenism in the area of sacramental theology, we must turn to the remarkable transformation that has taken place in our understanding of the Eucharist.

In the Middle Ages the theology of the Eucharist as sacrifice was comparatively undeveloped. St. Thomas and the important authors of his century paid special attention to Christ's real presence in the Eucharist and attempted to find a rational formulation which would shed some light upon the mysterious mode of this presence and thus protect it from material and superstitious interpretations. The theology of the Mass, however, was considered rather briefly; Thomas devoted only a single article to it in the *Summa*. In passing, however, he refers to the celebration of the Eucharist throughout his treatise on the sacraments.

That the Mass is a sacrifice was no theological problem for St. Thomas. Again and again he mentions that the eucharistic celebration is a sacrifice because it contains the passion of Christ. It is a sacrifice because it is a memorial of the death of the Lord and renders present the saving power of this event.

The Protestant Reformation rejected with indignation the ancient liturgy of the Mass. The polemics of the Reformers were especially directed against the notion of a eucharistic sacrifice. According to the Scriptures, they believed, there was only one sacrifice in the Church and this was the death of Jesus on the cross; and hence the multiplication of sacrifices on Catholic altars was to them an outrage, an insult to the uniqueness of Christ's death, and a mockery of almighty God. The Reformers regarded the Mass as a human thing, and consequently to ascribe to it redemptive power, as Catholics did, was a return to the paganism of antiquity.

To answer these terrible accusations, the simple theology of the Mass known in the Middle Ages was no longer adequate. The Council of Trent spent a whole session, the twenty-second, on the elaboration of an authoritative explanation of what the Mass is, but while the ancient Catholic doctrine was defined and vindicated, many important theological issues were left wideopen. The Church, after all, cannot produce theological insights at will; if the time is not ripe, if the subject has not matured in the minds of her doctors, she may indicate directions in which the answers must be found, yet be unable to resolve all the difficulties. Thus the Council of Trent had declared that in the sacrifice of the Mass the same Christ is contained and sacrificed who offered himself once and for all on the altar of the cross. The Council taught that the Mass is the same sacrifice as that of the cross, because in both we have the same divine victim, and the same divine Priest. Calvary and the Mass differ only in the way of offering: on Calvary Christ was killed, while in the Mass Christ is offered in an unbloody manner.

The Council of Trent, then, defined that the Mass is the same sacrifice as that of the cross, but it did not determine whether or not it is *numerically* the same sacrifice. It did not settle the relationship between the cross and the altar. It left room for a great deal of free speculation. The theologians of the Counter Reformation elaborated a theology of the Mass which, alas, was largely determined by apologetical preoccupations. Their concern was not how to become more faithful to the biblical teaching on the Eucharist, nor to learn from the eucharistic doctrine of the Fathers; rather, they tried to establish a more solid rational basis for the doctrine that the Mass is really a propitiatory sacrifice and that the minister of the Eucharist is truly a priest. The writers of that period had little sympathy with the agonizing scruples of Protestants who desired to save at all costs the uniqueness of Christ's sacrifice on the cross and the fullness of redemption he had acquired through his holy death. Thus the Catholic theologians walked a new way, unknown in Catholic tradition. Studying pre-Christian and non-Christian religions to discover the nature of sacrifice in general, they came to the conclusion that sacrifice always implied the destruction of a victim. Unless an offering to a divinity be destroyed, at least in part, one cannot properly speak of a sacrifice. With this theory in mind these theologians set out "to prove" that the Mass really and truly fulfills the requirements of a sacrifice. They tried to find a ritual destruction of some kind in the eucharistic liturgy of the Catholic Church. Some authors regarded Communion as the destruction of the sacred host; others preferred to think of the breaking of the host, others again of the double consecration. Some theologians thought of the consecration as the mystical immolation of Christ separating his blood from his body; others again asserted that Christ suffered some humiliation in his sacramental state, either by becoming food capable of being consumed, or by being confined behind the appearances of bread. For this group of writers the eucharistic celebration was a sacrifice because of a sacrificial destruction apart from Christ's death on the cross. These theologians still regarded the Mass and Calvary as the same sacrifice—priest and victim were the same in both—but this identity was specific, not numerical. They believed that each new ritual destruction repeated in some sense the sacrifice of Christ on the cross.

Another group of writers, especially Suarez, moved still further away from the ancient Catholic tradition and the Bible. Suarez believed that it was not necessary to have a ritual destruction in the eucharistic sacrifice. According to him, all that was required for a true sacrifice was the offering of a sacred thing to God. Thus he regarded the Mass as a sacrifice because the priest transformed bread and wine into the body and blood of Christ and then offered them ritually to God in the liturgy. In this theology the sacrifice of the Mass is numerically *and* specifically distinct from that of the cross. On Calvary Christ offered himself to the Father; but in the Mass, according to this theology, Christ present on the altar is offered to the Father by a human priest. If such a doctrine were preached, the faithful might be led to believe that the elevation of host and chalice after the consecration was a sacrificial gesture of the priest offering Christ to the Father. This would be superstition.

Today these theories sound rather fantastic, and we wonder how Christian men could have formulated doctrines which are so obviously at odds with the Scriptures. The one-sided apologetical approach blinded these authors in all the areas of controversy.

In our own century a Catholic theology of the Eucharist has been wonderfully renewed. The approach of the Baroque theologians has almost completely disappeared. To seek in the eucharistic liturgy a sacrificial destruction independent from that of the cross, is regarded as irreconcilable with the uniqueness of Christ's sacrifice on the cross and his glorified humanity after the resurrection. If the Mass is a sacrifice, and on this the tradition of the Church is unanimous, it must be because of a very special relationship to Christ's self-surrender on Calvary.

Early in this century, a few authors, such as De la Taille and Lepin, began to speak of an eternal sacrifice of Christ, a sacrifice beginning with his birth, leading to a climax on the cross, and made perpetual by his unceasing intercession in heaven. This was an approach quite at home in Anglican theology. These writers believed that through his resurrection and ascension Christ assumed an eternal victimhood in heaven. According to them, the Mass was a sacrificial celebration because the Church appropriated and made her own Christ's perpetual self-surrender before God. Christ's everlasting gift of himself to the Father which began at the moment of his human existence and continues to all eternity, becomes ours at Mass, and we are allowed to share in this heavenly sacrifice of charity and worship. Despite the limitations of this theory, it had the great advantage of seeking to explain the Church's eucharistic doctrine by emphasizing the initerable character of Christ's sacrifice. The work of De la Taille and Lepin had a liberating effect on Catholic eucharistic theology.

Since that time Catholic theologians have reflected very deeply on the eucharistic sacrifice. A return to the theological world of St. Thomas was a great step forward. Thomas's teaching on the Eucharist was simple and evangelical. He studied the Eucharist as a part of his general theology of the sacraments. Since the *Summa* regards a sacrament as a sacred sign announcing an act of Christ and applying it to those who receive it in faith, the doctrine that the Eucharist is a sacrifice can only mean that it is a sign of a sacrifice, of Christ's sacrifice, rendering present its redemptive power. As we have mentioned, for St. Thomas the Eucharist is a sacrifice simply because it is a memorial of Christ's death on Calvary and makes available the total power of Christ's sacrificial act to those who take part in it.

Various theologians have further refined this evangelical theology of St. Thomas, some by remaining altogether within a scholastic framework, others by enriching the notion of memorial or *anamnesis* from an analysis of Scripture. The tendency in contemporary eucharistic theologies, and there are many of them, is without doubt to show that the sacrifice of the Mass is the same as that of the cross. There is no repetition or renewal of Calvary in the Mass. What is repeated in Holy Mass is the Last Supper; the cross is initerable. Christ's death cannot be renewed, though it becomes effective again in the eucharistic celebration. Catholic writers speak of a re-presentation of the sacrifice of Calvary during Mass, or of a new presence of the cross as the celebration of the Eucharist. Such men as Vonier, Masure, and Journet have influenced the Catholic public to such an extent that this new, though traditional, theology has replaced the approaches of the Counter Reformation.

It should be pointed out that the liturgical movement has been an important factor in the evolution of this eucharistic theology. The liturgists were largely responsible for introducing the people to the ancient though neglected notion that at Mass they were in some sense witnesses and sharers in the sacrifice of Christ. Without offering them any particular theology, they simply proposed the ancient faith of the Church that Christ left the eucharistic celebration to the community so that the power of his cross be available at all times and that all generations implicate themselves in his own life-bringing sacrifice. Even if many writers disagree with Dom Odo Casel's understanding of how this mysterious sharing takes place, all liturgists profess and teach that during the Mass the sacrifice of Christ becomes present to us in such a way that we may be drawn into it, surrendering ourselves with Christ, and by assenting to the Lord drawing us we become offerers of his own redemptive sacrifice.

In these pages we have briefly traced the great change in the theology of the Eucharist that has taken place in our century. While we do not claim that this is exclusively due to ecumenism and dialogue with Protestant theologians, there can be no doubt that the ecumenical approach was an important factor in this evolution. It opened the way to a new freedom. It convinced theologians that they could leave the old apologetical positions without appearing disloyal. It taught them a new and more profound way of defending the Church. What the Catholic theologian wants to show is that the teaching of the Church is in harmony, not with a few quotations from the Bible, but with the total spirit of the inspired Scriptures; he desires to demonstrate that the legitimate complaints of Protestants have had their beneficial effect on us and that their truly evangelical aspirations —in this case, the sufficiency and uniqueness of Christ's work—are truly preserved and appreciated in the Catholic Church.

Are Protestant Christians sensitive to this evolution of our eucharistic understanding? The answer is Yes. Their theologians can now read our eucharistic theology and understand what we are trying to say. They have repeatedly expressed their sympathy with the liturgical movement and with the biblical rethinking of our sacramental practice. More than that, we shall show in the following pages that the ecumenical dialogue which has had a significant effect on us, has also stimulated a parallel evolution in Protestant sacramental theology.

In the areas of doctrine and life touched upon in this chapter, we have noted significant changes within the Catholic Church. In passing, we have referred to new church architecture and to the revival of a biblical-liturgical piety among Catholics, even outside the Church's official worship. We have paid more attention to various aspects of Catholic sacramental theology and in each case have observed a remarkable evolution produced, at least in part, through the ecumenical approach. It is most encouraging that in these same areas of doctrine and life a parallel transformation has taken place among Protestant Christians, at least among those who are touched by the ecumenical movement. We have already mentioned their new church architecture. In the field of prayer, piety and worship, the great Protestant Churches have made tremendous strides in recent decades. I am not speaking of such happy extremes as the return to monastic life among the Lutherans and Calvinists of Europe; rather, I am referring to the more universal attempt in all the Churches to purify their prayers, public and private, of sentimentality and individualism, which had been a danger to Protestantism in the past, and to rediscover a liturgical worship containing the great redemptive and sacramental themes of the Scriptures. That the liturgical movement affects sacramental practice *and* the pattern of spiritual life has been the common experience of Catholics and Protestants in our century.

Our age has seen among the Protestant Churches a revival of sacramental thinking which is without parallel in their history. One of the reasons for this is the new biblical scholarship, which has demonstrated that sacramental life is deeply rooted in divine revelation itself. Many parts of the Scriptures must be understood in the liturgical context in which they were written. A still more powerful factor for this sacramental revival is undoubtedly the ecumenical movement. We have mentioned that ecumenism, far from encouraging indifferentism in faith, actually draws attention to the central themes of the gospel and focuses special concern on the very areas where the Churches differ. The sacraments, especially the Eucharist, contain a divine message regarding Christian unity. They announce the unity which the community of Christ has received and is meant to possess, and they denounce the divisions which, despite this gift, keep Christians apart. This message is keenly felt at all the meetings of the World Council of Churches, where the unity of intention and hope in Christ never becomes manifest in a common sacramental worship. This problem of intercommunion, as it is called, is the most anguishing one of the Protestant ecumenical community.

Protestant Christians are well aware of the sacramental evolution within their Churches. It is too obvious to miss. A glance at the books published, the preoccupation of theologians, and the liturgical renewals in all the Churches touched by ecumenism will convince us of the power of this new trend. On the level of theology and official teaching, the development is so universal —even if it has not reached all ministers and the whole people— that it is hard to choose, among so many, one single quotation from Protestant sources to convince the Catholic reader. I wish to quote a beautiful passage from the introduction to the sacraments in the new *Manual of Church Doctrine According to the Church of Scotland:*

In order to our salvation the Eternal Word "became flesh" and dwelt among us, taking our nature in its completeness—body, soul and spirit—into union with His Deity, to become the instrument of our regeneration. Through the humanity thus assumed God "took hold" of our nature to redeem and refashion it. . . . [In the sacraments] he comes to us under the sign and veil of physical objects especially appointed by him to represent him and specially sanctified by him as instruments of his self-communication. In the sacraments therefore Christ assumes a sensible vehicle and, in association with sign and element for our recognition and appreciation, wants us to share in the mystery of the incarnate life and death and resurrection. The sacraments result from the fact that salvation operates by incarnation; and they import that our relation to Christ is a living relation embracing our whole nature, bodily as well as spiritual.

Reading these magnificent sentences, Catholics will be surprised and staggered. This is not what they had imagined Calvinism to be. It is true, of course, that this is not what Calvinism has been for some time, but the ecumenical movement has made itself felt within all the Calvinist Churches and transformed them considerably. The sacraments have again become a Christian reality in the Protestant ecumenical community.

Since we have paid special attention to Catholic eucharistic theology, we wish to take a closer look at its Protestant counterpart. Do we find there an analogous evolution? We recall that one of the great objections of the Reformers against the Church, an objection propounded in the most vehement fashion, was to the Catholic notion of eucharistic sacrifice. The Reformers argued that a sacrificial understanding of the Eucharist was irreconcilable with the all-sufficiency of the cross of Christ. Luther, who retained the notion of Christ's real presence in the Eucharist, rejected the Mass of the Catholic Church as an abomination. For Luther the Mass was a human work, and hence to regard it as a sacrifice and means of salvation was not only a superstition but an act of pride, a bold gesture of man seeking to intrude upon the divine economy of mercy. In the Anglican Church, too, the Reformation rejected the idea of a eucharistic sacrifice, except as the self-oblation of the communicant. When Anglican theologians in the seventeenth century returned to a more traditional appreciation of Christ's real presence in the Eucharist, they still hesitated to reintroduce the sacrificial understanding of the liturgy. It was only the Oxford movement of the nineteenth century that restored the Eucharist as an atoning sacrifice in the Anglican Church. At that time this sacrificial interpretation was regarded as thoroughly un-Protestant, both by the people who advocated it and by those who fought against it. The eucharistic theology of the Oxford movement exerted no influence whatever on the authentic Protestant traditions within and without the Church of England. Until quite recently the indignant rejection of the Mass as a sacrificial eucharistic celebration belonged to the very essence of Protestantism.

In our day the Faith and Order movement, one of the main currents of the whole Protestant ecumenical movement, has affected a considerable change in this situation. The Conference of Edinburgh (1937) marked the beginning of a new development. The final report of this Conference, approved by all members, outlined a eucharistic doctrine which was strongly influenced by Anglican theology. Bishop Hicks, an Anglican theologian of distinction, had given a paper to the assembly which was regarded as so significant that it was appended to the official report. Bishop Hicks had proposed two points. He claimed that on the one hand the notion of eucharistic sacrifice against which the Reformers had protested was really a medieval theological corruption, and on the other hand there was a biblical idea of sacrifice associated with the Eucharist which the Reformers had overlooked in the heat of the arguments.

This provocative statement stimulated a great deal of research in all the Protestant Churches. In his own paper, Bishop Hicks had proposed the theory that Christ offers a continuous sacrifice to his Father, first on earth through his life and death and later in heaven, as head of the Church, through his loving surrender as perpetual victim. It is this permanent sacrifice of Christ which becomes available to the Church in the Eucharist; and by letting herself be drawn into Christ's self-surrender, his gift of himself to the Father becomes also hers. Hicks speaks therefore of the Eucharist as the sacrifice of the Church.

Such an analysis of the eucharistic celebration was not acceptable to all Protestant theologians. Although Hicks was the spokesman for an influential group of Anglicans (men like A. G. Hebert, Gregory Dix, and Arthur Ramsey, the present Archbishop of Canterbury, would be in agreement with such a eucharistic theology), the more traditionally Protestant theologians could not but reject this theory utterly and completely. As a matter of fact, the majority of Catholic theologians also reject the idea of a perpetual sacrifice of Christ: The risen *Kyrios* is now no longer victim.

When the Faith and Order movement met again in 1952, this time in Lund, Sweden, the entire subject of liturgy and sacrament had been carefully prepared. A series of books had been published containing theological studies of different confessional viewpoints. Much theological and historical research had been carried on by several scholars and published in book form or in various scholarly journals. In the minutes of the Lund Conference we read the following observation, startling though it may seem, on the theological conversations dealing with the Eucharist: "We reached in our discussion a measure of understanding, which none of us could have anticipated, on the problem of the sacrificial element in holy communion."

This is not the place to discuss the various eucharistic theologies Protestant authors have produced in recent decades. Some of them follow the Anglican theme of the perpetual sacrifice of Christ, into which the Church enters through the Eucharist. Others, especially Lutherans, emphasize the presence of the glorious Christ in the Eucharist, accompanied by his entire redemptive work. Others again have developed the biblical notion of *anamnesis* and teach that the sacrifice on Calvary is alive in its memorial, the eucharistic celebration. All I wish to do in this chapter is to present a number of significant quotations from Protestant theologians which will convince the reader of the seriousness of their theological quest, the ecumenical and self-critical character of their approach, and the return to greater orthodoxy as a result of the ecumenical dialogue.

This is what the German Lutheran theologian Stählin writes on the Eucharist:

Since 1526 (when Luther wrote the German Mass) the Lutheran Church has shown an almost ineradicable suspicion concerning the very idea of sacrifice in the Eucharist, for fear that the emphasis on man's sacrificial activity might obscure the exclusiveness of the divine gift of grace, which we human beings can only gratefully receive and accept. In present discussions among Lutheran theologians in Germany there are not a few who demand the reinstitution of sacrifice to its due place within Christian worship.

A similar position is taken by the Swedish Lutheran theologian Brilioth:

In Luther's day controversial needs rendered it impossible that he should allow any place to the Eucharist as *anamnesis*. But the case is different today. Today the enemy is no longer the Roman canon and the abuses that followed in its train, but rather the impoverishment of faith and of worship in our own ranks. The Church of today has no grounds for refusing a place to this side of the Eucharist. Rather she needs to aim at recovering the evangelical conception of the sacrament in its completeness, drawing out the implications of Luther's own teaching and ancient Lutheran practice.

Summing up his positive doctrine on the sacrificial aspects of the eucharistic celebration, the Danish Lutheran theologian Prenter declares that "the Eucharist is the eternal presence in the Church of the sacrifice of Calvary." Similarly, the Swedish Lutheran theologian Aulén concludes his study on the Eucharist with these words:

"The real presence and the sacrifice belong together. This sacrifice is present because the living Lord is present. But the living Lord cannot be present without actualizing his sacrifice. Because he is the *living* Lord who unites us with his sacrifice, he also makes us partakers of his victory."

After these voices from Lutheranism, let us listen to Calvinist theologians. Their tradition is further away from a sacramental appreciation than is that of the Lutherans, and yet even here the ecumenical dialogue, a freer return to the Scriptures, and the practice of the Church have produced a remarkable change of outlook.
The Dutch Calvinist Van der Leeuw writes:

The idea of re-presentation as it is advocated in many circles nowadays, Roman Catholic, Anglican, as well as Lutheran, also seems to present some perspectives for future development of sacramental theology for the Reformed Churches. The central sacrament, the Eucharist, is not a repetition of Christ's sacrifice, neither is it simply a making mention of it in a solemn way. But it is the re-presentation of the act of God on Calvary.

The German Reformed theologian Graf has this to say about the Eucharist: "The Church does not simply remember the death of the Lord: She re-presents the sacrifice itself, letting herself enter into the suffering and death of Christ, into his obedience." The well-known Scottish Presbyterian theologian Torrance sums up his eucharistic theology in these sentences: "The Eucharist is the sacramental counterpart of the unique sacrifice of Christ, and therefore in its own way, inasmuch as it echoes that, and is derivative from it, a sacramental sacrifice. In reality it is Christ who in the Eucharist represents to the Church and makes effective for the Church his own atoning deed of sacrifice."

The Calvinist theologian Leenhardt of Geneva writes in his study of the Last Supper that the Eucharist is "more than a commemoration." He continues: "The redemptive past becomes the present of faith. What God has done once, he continues to do. When it is said that God acted once for all, this does not mean that he ceased to act. The action of God (in Christ's sacrifice) is continuous in all the acts which prolong it and realize it again."

This remarkable transformation observable in the great theological traditions of separated Western Christianity has had some influence on the nonconformist Churches. In a report *The Catholicity of Protestantism,* prepared by a group of English ministers representing the Free Churches, we read that the Lord's Supper

is not merely a solemn reminder of Christ's sacrifice of himself, the sacrifice which was "once offered" on the cross. It is the dramatic setting forth of that sacrifice, and the means whereby we can participate in it and all its benefits. For in the sacrament, the crucified and risen Savior himself is present with us to impart to us a share in all that is his.

The above quotations are clear and outspoken. While they may surprise many churchgoing Protestants, they are truly representative of the spiritual atmosphere of contemporary Protestant theology. As we shall see later, the Protestantism of North America differs considerably from that of Europe, and hence it is only fair to say that the development in eucharistic theology we have described is more pronounced on the continent of Europe. Signs are not lacking, however, that these trends are beginning to influence American Protestantism. With the increase of ecumenical interest among American Protestants, we may expect a more orthodox understanding of the role of the sacraments in the Christian Church. It is worth noting in this connection that the American reticence in regard to ecumenism is found among Protestants and Catholics alike, and that the circles in opposition to ecumenism are also those that reject the liturgical movement, the new biblical understanding of the sacraments, and the renewal of theology begun by the great European authors.

The beautiful quotations given above should not lead us to the conclusion that they teach a truly Catholic doctrine of the Eucharist. Sentences which sound perfectly orthodox to us may still be interpreted in an un-Catholic way. Nor must we think that these theologians are on the way to becoming Catholics. The idea most probably has never even entered their heads. What takes place in them is a deeper understanding of their own Protestant tradition, purified of its exaggerations and enriched by greater conformity to the Bible.

What is the attitude of the Catholic when faced with such a serious attempt to appreciate the fullness of the eucharistic gifts? Some of us might be tempted to pass these things off as irrelevant because the eucharistic celebration of Protestants is not valid. This would be utterly wrong. According to Catholic theology, the sacrament of the Eucharist is absolutely necessary for holiness and transformation in Christ. St. Thomas especially emphasized that for the full and vital integration of men in Christ the Eucharist is an absolutely necessity. For Catholics there exists the vital need to participate in the Mass and to receive Holy Communion *in re*. Those who are prevented from sharing the Eucharist *in re*, for whatever reason, must share in it *in voto*. They must desire, according to the insight they have received, to partake of the gift of the Eucharist, which is the new life in Christ imparted to the entire community. Thomas does not explain how these supernatural desires arise in those outside the Church, how these desires are expressed, or what precise form they take. But for separated Christians there is surely no more effective way of receiving the Eucharist *in voto* than by taking part in their own eucharistic liturgies. For men inspired by faith, good will, and charity, these eucharistic liturgies, though inadequate from the strictly sacramental point of view, become precious means of grace and an invisible sharing in the full fruit of the sacramental mystery. Cardinal Newman believed that a communion service of unordained ministers offered "quasi-sacramental grace" to the faithful taking part in it with eucharistic faith. A Catholic would be untheological and disloyal if he despised or belittled the worship of separated Christians; but he does not take part in it, since he has access to the realities which his dissident brethren seek.

In this chapter we have shown how the ecumenical dialogue, producing a new outlook and leading to more profound research, has initiated considerable changes in the eucharistic theology of Catholics and Protestants. Without any compromise, without any wishy-washiness, we have come closer to one another. Similar movements could have been described in other areas of Church doctrine and life. Many Protestant Churches have been led back to greater orthodoxy and a more traditional understanding of the gospel of Christ, and the Catholic Church herself has discovered a more balanced possession of all her gifts and a more impartial expression of her wisdom.

7

THE FACE OF PROTESTANTISM

SINCE OUR LOVE is not authentic unless we try to understand our friends, the new ecumenical charity demands that Catholics show some understanding of the Protestant Christianity surrounding them. It is not easy to have insight into the beliefs of others. The ordinary Catholic is not called to be a scholar. But we can all learn to become aware of the variety of trends within Protestantism and thus avoid the sweeping statements concerning Protestants in general when we only refer to one tendency among them.

Our terminology in regard to Protestants is revealing. In the ecumenical dialogue the use of words counts. Take, for example, the words *heretic* and *heretical*. They are ancient Christian words which cannot be removed from the Christian vocabulary, nor indeed from Christian experience. In Scripture we are told that false teachers will come, that they will disturb the community, announce a message at variance with the gospel preached by the apostles, and draw along with them into perdition those who refuse to listen to the Church. The classical meaning of heretic always refers to men who are guilty of sin, that is, to men who knowingly and wilfully reject the faith of the Christian community. An heretical doctrine, in the ancient sense, was one which was not only at variance with orthodoxy but was also obstinately upheld against the authority of the Church. Heretical was always a term of total condemnation, referring to the most terrible thing a man could do: to sin against faith.

However, in more recent centuries we have begun to use the word heretical rather differently. We have applied it to Protestants (and their teaching) whether they were guilty of sin or not. The word began to stand for error in doctrine, while traditionally it had always referred to a sinful situation. The new usage signified a fault in the intellectual order, while the ancient usage referred to a fault principally in the order of the will and charity. Softening our way of speaking in more recent years, we began to refer to Protestants born and brought up outside the Church as "heretics in good faith," a most unfortunate expression completely against classical usage. A man in good faith is simply not a heretic, just as a man who accidently gives wrong information is not a liar. More is required for men to be liars or heretics than to err in the mind; there must be malice in the will.

In our own day we have gone back to the original usage of the term. We do not refer to Protestant Christians as heretics or to their teachings as heretical. They may become heretics and their teachings may be heretical: this happens whenever they knowingly oppose the divine guidance coming to them from the Christian community, the Church. But unless we wish to accuse them of this kind of bad faith, the word simply should not be used. It is insulting. It offends against truth and charity. It is worthy of note that the official documents of the Holy See since Leo XIII never refer to Protestant Christians as heretics. The word *heretical* is still used—the heretical spirit is a reality found among Catholics and Protestants—but it is never applied to separated Christians who are heirs of their dissidence. They are simply called dissident Christians. It is a basic rule of ecumenical charity never to use the word heretical except in the ancient meaning, and never to apply it to Protestant Christians whom we believe to be in good faith.

Another word which frequently offends Protestant Christians is sect or sectarian. In a certain kind of Catholic literature all Protestant Churches and denominations are referred to as sects, whether they belong to the sectarian tradition or not. When the late Archbishop of Chicago wrote his pastoral letter on the occasion of the Second Assembly of the World Council of Churches at Evanston, he spoke of the assembled Churches as "sects" and thereby greatly offended many Protestant Christians. We shall have to say more about sects and Churches later on. At this point we simply wish to recall that in the sixteenth century the Reformation of Luther and Calvin and the separation of the Anglican Church were accompanied by another religious phenomenon, the rise of sectarian movements in violent opposition to all Churches, Catholic and Protestant. The sects were characterized by particular doctrines making them enemies alike of Catholics and Protestants, and it would be unhistorical and quite unkind to identify Protestant Churches with the sects against which they have defended the principles of orthodoxy for centuries.

Sometimes Catholics refer to Protestant Churches as sects because they believe that a high loyalty to their own Church demands this. There is only one Church, the Catholic Church, and hence how can we call other Christian communities Churches? The same kind of Catholic would never call a presbyter of the Anglican Church a priest nor address him as Father, fearing that he would thereby be disloyal to Leo XIII's declaration on the invalidity of Anglican orders. Such an attitude is ridiculous. It is true that in a highly theological context one would confuse the issue by not using a terminology that was dogmatically correct, but in ordinary situations of life the elementary rule of charity and mutual respect is that we refer to others, and to what is sacred to them, by the words which they themselves prefer to use. Even quite apart from a deeper reason, we must call Protestant Churches Churches and Anglican priests priests, just as we find it quite natural that a non-Catholic addresses a Catholic priest as Father, though in his eyes he is no father at all. Our fussiness with words, our fears of applying to others words which are only meant for ourselves, actually corresponds not to a Catholic, but to a sectarian, mentality. The sectarian, as we shall see, is constantly preoccupied with his own election and resists intermingling and identification with others. The sectarian is slow to recognize good will in others, unless they want to be regenerated in his own group.

It is perhaps worthwhile to mention here the widespread custom in English-speaking lands, even among ecumenically minded Protestants, of referring to the Church as the *Roman* Catholic Church. It is true that we are the Roman Church. The visible head of the Church is the Bishop of Rome, and being in union with the See of Rome is the sign and seal of true Church membership. But to have oneself always referred to as Roman Catholic is unpleasant. It is a custom which does not exist in other languages. The reason why Protestant ecumenists in the English-speaking world will rarely speak of the Catholic Church without qualification, is the claim of the Anglican Church to be the Catholic Church as well. With all respect for this Anglican conviction, it must be nevertheless admitted that the Anglican Church has not always cherished the name of Catholic, that for many centuries its members did not think of themselves as Catholics, and that even today many Anglicans refuse to think of themselves as Catholics. It would be more generous on the part of Anglicans and ecumenical Protestants to recognize the priority of this name to the papal Church and simply refer to her as the Catholic Church. The Eastern Churches not in union with Rome call themselves Orthodox, and though the Catholic Church also claims to be orthodox, it would be unkind if Catholics began to call themselves Orthodox and refer to the Churches of the East only as Eastern-Orthodox. There are certain historical rights to titles.

Ecumenical charity, however, is not confined to the proper use of words. We cannot love Protestant Christians unless we have some true knowledge of them. If we are left to the odd pieces of information picked up in films, novels, and plays, or if we simply base our notions on our own experience with a few Protestant friends, our picture must be one-sided and hence not without danger. Too many Catholics regard Protestants as men whose sole principle is that of private interpretation. The Protestant reads the Bible and makes his own religion; he follows his own personal preferences. The Protestant, according to this popular prejudice, may be either a liberal person concerned with helping his neighbor and not caring much about divine religion, or a fanatical upholder of a homemade creed, an aggressive fundamentalist, unlearned and bigoted.

To gain some understanding of dissident Christianity, we must look at four different currents within the Protestant tradition, which in various proportions and different intensities make up the Protestant world. Occasionally we find Catholic books trying to describe Protestantism by giving an account, alphabetically arranged, of the various Protestant denominations and Churches. This approach does not give much light. This method is insensitive to the fact that the significant divisions of Protestantism cut right across denominational boundaries. The well-known Scottish theologian Torrance begins the second volume of his *Conflict and Agreement in the Church* with this sentence: "It is increasingly evident today that the lines of conflict and agreement in the Church coincide less and less with the frontiers of the historic Communions." The alphabetical approach does not really help us to understand the deep things Protestants believe, or to discover the areas where they are faithful to the Word of God, and where, in the eyes of Catholics, they go astray. By listing the various denominations alphabetically, first Adventists, then Anglicans, then Baptists, and so on, we create the impression that these groups are equivalent species of the same genus Protestantism, thereby obscuring the great supernatural differences between Churches and sects. This method is often quite offensive to Protestants and hence also to ecumenically minded Catholics.*

We shall now give a brief description of the four currents in the Protestant tradition. The first and principal area we must examine is the theological outlook created by the original Reformers, Luther and Calvin. The Lutheran and Calvinistic Churches have undergone many transformations throughout the centuries, but a stream of orthodox Protestantism has always remained in them. Especially in our own time, this spirit has been renewed and purified by the neo-orthodox theology which has changed the face of continental Protestantism.

How are we to describe the spirit of orthodox Protestantism? Its first and foremost characteristic is the extreme emphasis on the sovereignty of God and the divine initiative in human life. God acts in history to save those he loves, he intervenes sovereignly to justify the sinner who has turned his back on him. In Jesus Christ he crosses the abyss which separates his own eternal glory for small and sinful men. Salvation therefore cannot be a joint affair between God and man; in the eyes of the Reformers, it is simply God's doing. God in Christ, lifting man up on his shoulder, carries him away to safety and joy. Hence, whatever a man does, or tries to do, in this holy process will count against him. He must simply trust in the God who takes hold of him. The easiest way of being lifted up to anyone's shoulder is by keeping still and trustingly to follow the strong movement of the other.

This sounds quite biblical so far, except for the tendency to regard man too exclusively in his impotence. For the Reformers man was so small before God and so sinful in his heart, that he was radically incapable of responding to God's grace in adequate proportion. Man was not only a sinner prior to his encounter

---

* There is no English introduction to Protestantism as useful and reliable as George Tavard's modest volume called *Protestantism*. The author gives real insight into the heart of the Protestant tradition and successfully avoids the statistical and sociological approach.

with the saving God; even after this event, he remained marked
by a fundamental ambiguity. God was forever working in man,
but all the works of man were marked by the ambivalence of
his own heart. There was no ideal of perfect sanctity to which
the justified have access, and hence the active striving for a life
transformed and purified in grace was regarded as pride, seeking
justice by works, or monkish asceticism. Not that the Reformers
failed to urge their followers to advance in virtue! They did,
but the growth in moral perfection was not regarded as part of
the redemptive process going on in man. It did not bring him
closer to God, it did not establish in him a greater share in the
life of Christ.

We find in the Reformers a tendency toward a holy skepticism.
The sovereignty of God gave them an abiding sense of the relative in all things human and created. There was no absolute
standard, except the eternal and incomprehensible God; and anything below God claiming to be an absolute offered the constant
temptation of idolatry. Even the holiest things, such as the Church
and her creed, sent by God and established for our salvation, were
ultimately relative and provisional, and retained the character of
the ambiguous. Considered as an absolute, even the Church presented the temptation of idolatry. The Reformers did not wish to
reject Church order and sacraments, nor did they intend to
overthrow an established hierarchy; but their prophetic vision of
God's incommunicable sovereignty made them reject the Catholic
notion that God has committed himself definitively to human
forms, historical institutions, to words and signs. The Reformers
wanted to retain the order of the Church, only to move it altogether into the realm of the humanly conditioned.

The ultimate guarantee that God is on our side is only found
in faith. There is nothing else, not even baptism, not the orthodoxy nor the pardon of the Church; only faith. Virtue, religious
experience, love of God, charity toward others—none of these
gives me access to the mercy of God; for these are always tainted

by my impotence, even when God is with me. Only my faith, the recognition that I am incapable of saving myself and the willingness to rely utterly and entirely on God's mercy revealed in Christ, only this confidence gives me access to salvation. Faith, for the Reformers, was not an act or a deed meriting salvation; it was precisely the abdication of man before God, the recognition that alone he was helpless, that there was no human hope, that there was only God who justified the sinner.

The Catholic will object here that it is precisely the scandal of the gospel that God linked himself irrevocably to human things and to a community of men, and that therefore the area of history touched by God's Incarnation loses the conditional character proper to the created order.

For Protestants, though deeply respectful of the realities of the Church, the principal vehicle of God's redemptive power was the Word of God, in which the almighty and merciful Lord revealed himself, and by revealing himself took hold of those listening in faith. This Word of God was present to us in the Bible. For the Reformers the Bible was not identified with God's Word—this narrow biblicist view is an invention of the sects—but the Bible was rather the area where the sovereign Word encountered man, judged and redeemed him, comforted and reprimanded him. In this view the ecclesiastical realities became secondary and relative. Against Luther's intention, this doctrine destroyed the Church to which he belonged, and he became obliged to build up one of his own. He tried to take up the elements of traditional Christianity, but he translated them all into a new conditional tense. Ultimately, only God's Word was relevant.

This absolute sufficiency of unpredictable grace is the most typically Protestant attitude. Persons in contact only with American Protestantism in a practical way might not always be aware of this. The spirit of Lutheranism and the more orthodox aspects of Calvinism have not deeply marked American religion. On our continent Protestantism has become more subjective and more moral than was the highly prophetical faith of the early Reformers.

The second area of Protestantism we must briefly describe is the Anglican world. There was a time when Anglicans preferred to be considered Protestants; yet according to an ever-growing movement within their Church, in England and abroad, they prefer to think of themselves as both Protestant and Catholic, but especially as Catholic. And they have good reason for doing so. At the time of the Reformation two radical changes took place in England, the first the Church's secession from the See of Rome under Henry VIII, and the second the influx of continental Protestantism under Edward and Elizabeth. While the Church of England remained faithful to ancient Catholic tradition after the schism under Henry, the Reformation under his successors tried to suppress many elements of Catholic creed and sacramental life. From that time on, there have existed in the Church of England two traditions side by side, in varying proportions, one essentially Catholic, the other truly Protestant in inspiration. For either spiritual or political reasons, it was the Catholic tendency which was usually dominant in England, and hence throughout the centuries the emphatically Protestant movements, such as the Puritans, the Methodists, and other Free Churches, separated themselves from the established Church. Since the Oxford movement or Tractarianism (which has become famous among Catholics through the person of Newman), the orthodox trend in the Anglican Church has continually grown in strength. Today the vitality of Anglicanism, the new ideas, and the great literature seem to come from the Catholic wing of the Church of England, even if the majority of its adherents, especially in North America, are quite Protestant in outlook.

In contrast to the marked individualism of the Reformers, Anglicans have always been conscious that God intervened in history to save a community. God in Jesus Christ has established a holy community on this earth, the earthly body of the Lord, in which the individual is to find his salvation. Anglicans believe that Christ gave to his apostles rites and ordinances through which this community was to endure in history. For Anglicans the Church is prior to the individuals who are saved in her. They believe as we do that Christ bound himself to historical institutions. Christ, as the first-born of many brethren, wanted to be surrounded by a holy community praising God the Father with him, a community passing on through the centuries a creed, the sacraments, and holy orders to create new worshipers with him for God. And yet the transcendence of this God is often so emphasized by Anglicans that the visible gifts of Christ tend to be regarded as ultimately relative compared to the sovereign saving action of God. For many Anglicans the visible links to Christ's body on earth are important, but ultimately imprecise; a shade of indefiniteness covers even the creeds they profess and the orders they acknowledge. Despite their great attachment to the Christian tradition, Anglicans are constantly afraid that rigor in dogmatic formulas and insistence on institutions could be regarded by God as pride.

There is much in Anglicanism that is in complete harmony with the life of the Catholic Church, even if in our eyes their orders are not valid. It is surprising to find so little sympathy on the part of Catholics for Anglican contributions to theology. Although the liturgical and literary traditions within the Church of England are rich, beautiful, and extremely interesting, we have hardly ever studied them or made use of them in our own theological reflections. The friendly attitude of Pope John XXIII receiving in audience the Archbishop of Canterbury in December 1960 should do much to open the mind of Catholics to appreciate the positive elements in the Anglican tradition.

There is a third area of Protestantism which we must look at briefly. It is known under the name of "liberal." Protestant liberalism is a powerful movement which began in the last century in

Germany, when a number of important spiritual leaders detached themselves from the historic creeds of the Christian Church and defined religion in terms of personal experience. Religion was regarded by them as the feeling of utter dependence on God. In this view Jesus came to be a great prophet, a teacher of wisdom, who led men to the acknowledgment of God's fatherhood and the brotherhood of all men. This religious liberalism has existed under many different forms, has been couched in a variety of different theories, and has been influenced by diverse philosophical views; but all of its exponents are agreed in excluding the specifically supernatural from the Christian faith. In some the emphasis was more rational, and in others more emotional. This humanitarian religion successfully invaded the larger Churches of Europe and a little later found enthusiastic approval in Anglo-Saxon Protestantism, where the occasional vagueness of Anglicans and the emotionalism of the sects had already undermined the firm convictions of historical Christianity. There are vast numbers of Protestants in North America today who call themselves Christians but who have hardly retained any elements of traditional Christianity or of the Protestant Reformation.

By a curious shift of emphasis liberal Christianity proposes a world view which is almost diametrically opposed to the position of the Reformers. Instead of emphasizing divine transcendence, it tends to regard God as the good father indulgently smiling on his children, ready to help them to have happier and fuller lives. Instead of seeing humanity wounded by a radical guilt, the liberal Christian rejects the doctrine of original sin and regards human society as a rather pleasant group of men capable of being led to peace and contentment by an adequate system of education. In liberal Christianity there is no preoccupation with God, no emphasis on divine initiative, no doctrine of grace.

At the same time the liberals have made great contributions to the advance of Christianity. Our critical biblical and historical scholarship goes back to the scientific zeal of liberals. Even if we reject many of their conclusions, we certainly owe a good deal to them. The liberal, moreover, were convinced defenders of the freedom of religion; and here again the older Churches, whether Catholic or Protestant, had much to learn. Only after the liberal movement opened our eyes did we discover that religious freedom is a good firmly rooted in the Christian gospel. A third advance due to liberal Christianity is the social concern which has often been associated with it. While the older Churches, both Catholic and Protestant, tended to be conservative, the liberals in religion were often, though by no means always, engaged in the betterment of social conditions and human life. Here again God desired that his orthodox children be reminded by these men, many of them unbaptized or unchurched, that the Christian gospel implies a concern for social justice.

Through the influence of Karl Barth and other neo-orthodox theologians after him, Protestant liberalism has died among the spiritual leaders of Protestant Europe. In English-speaking lands the liberals are still quite influential. Yet in our day they are not very creative; they offer no new ideas, no significant message for our society; they have become respectable and uninteresting. By a curious transformation they are no longer the circles from which biblical and historical research receives a strong impetus, and they no longer have a special concern for social problems.

The fourth area at which we must look if we want to understand the Protestant world is the sectarian movement. We have already mentioned that in the sixteenth century, at the time of Luther and Calvin, another religious revolt took place with the appearance of the Anabaptist sects. These groups were in opposition to all organized Churches, Protestant as well as Catholic. They read the Bible in a simplistic fashion, guided neither by Christian tradition nor by personal learning. Carried away by religious enthusiasm, they become extremely otherworldly and at times apocalyptical in outlook and behavior. They tended to despise human reason and human culture, and sought to escape from the bondage of civilization by withdrawal and, occasionally, by violent political action. These unfortunate men, who usually came from the lowest social class, were persecuted by Churches and the heads of governments alike. Throughout the history of the Protestant Churches, sects sprang up in every century, reacting against traditional values and breaking away from the larger bodies. Since they were usually held in social disfavor, they emigrated in large numbers to North America. The specific tone of religion in North America is largely the creation of our sectarian past.

What was the particular Christian outlook of these sects? Their first characteristic was a theological individualism. They carried to their ultimate conclusions principles which the Reformers had proposed with qualifications. For them Jesus was the Savior entering a world lost in darkness and a humanity handed over to sin. Jesus alone saved. Clinging to him in faith and being thus cleansed by the blood of the Lamb, they were to separate themselves from a human society destined to destruction. The sectarians formed small groups in opposition to the established Churches. They refused to have anything to do with human institutions, with philosophy and culture. All was darkness in the world for them; only Jesus saved. Because of their distrust of the power of reason, they easily fell into enthusiasm, in an uncritical surrender to religious emotions. They clung most faithfully to a stern moral law, but they would not subject their spiritual experiences to the biblical tests and the guidance of the Christian community, which could distinguish true mystical inspirations from emotional upheavals and fanaticism.

This hostility to human culture became most evident in their use of Holy Scripture. They believed that the Bible was an easy book to read, that it was self-explanatory. Research and science were not really necessary. Each man was so guided by the Spirit that he would come to the true meaning of God's Word without the help of exegetical means and without the guidance of the Church. The famous principle of private interpretation, which is often called typically Protestant, really had its origin in the sectarian movement. It is not a principle at home in classical Protestantism. The Reformers never accepted any notion of private interpretation, even if they were unable to formulate a consistent doctrine of how to understand the Bible; that is, how much to rely on biblical science, and how much on the experience of the Christian community and the tradition of the Church. The antirational tendencies of the sects led them to a slavishly literal understanding of the sacred text, and thus they often arrived at conclusions which had little to do with the true meaning of Scripture.

The separation from the world sought by these sectarians was often symbolically expressed by special customs in food, drink, or clothing. These peculiarities became to them a sign of their own election, and they became extremely attached to them, as if these belonged to the heart of the Christian religion.

To the honor of these sects it must be said that they were largely inspired by evangelical ideals of simplicity, fraternity, and poverty. They reacted against everything that smacked of formalism. They gave up the liturgy for the sake of a more direct relationship with God. The fervor of enthusiasts is one of the most tragic phenomena of Christian history: men full of good will, afire with the spirit of sacrifice and an ardent love for Christ, and yet men fanatically blind to reality and hence also to the true meaning of the Word of God.

Because of the importance of the sects in North America, we should distinguish them more carefully from the Churches. The sects, we have said, are individualistic and exclusive. They believe that Jesus is the Savior of the few. These few, the chosen few, the group of the elect, withdraw from the common life of human society. The Churches, on the other hand, are social and inclusive in outlook. Jesus, according to their theology, is not the Savior of the few, but of the multitudes. The Lord came, not to separate the few from society, but to send the many into society in order to transform it. The Churches seek to penetrate an entire people. They desire to cover a whole territory, to embrace every single person of a given area, in order to create a new social structure reflecting, to some extent at least, the ideals of the gospel. The Churches preach a vision of Christianity which is not only interior but also seeks expression in cultural and political forms. Because of this open attitude the Churches have a positive outlook on human culture, on science, and the use of reason. Even when they are skeptical in regard to philosophy, the Churches always try to find a wide and coherent view of the universe in terms of biblical faith, and they are willing to make use of reason and scholarship in the elaboration of their theology. The sects, on the other hand, are profoundly antitheological. The Churches may shrink from a rigidly organized ecclesiastical structure, but they have always recognized the biblical role of hierarchy and order in the building up of the body of Christ. The sects, on the other hand, are anti-ecclesiastical. They resent the limitations imposed upon the individual, or the chapel, by the larger organism of the Christian community.

These differences between sects and Churches have created two entirely different religious and political mentalities. Wherever we find an uncritical, sentimental religion accompanied by a legalistic understanding of Christian morality, we recognize the fruits of a sectarian attitude. Certain phenomena frequently associated with fervent Christians, such as isolationism, indifference to things intellectual, and lack of sensitivity to art and human culture, are typical of the sectarian tradition.

We can now begin to understand how unjust and uncharitable it would be if we designated all Protestant Churches with the name of "sect." The traditional Protestant Churches have always rejected the sectarian spirit. In Europe, where these religious phenomena first developed, the distinction between Church and sect was so clear that one always knew what kind of Christian body one was facing. In America the religious situation is not as clear-cut. No writer has been more insistent than Reinhold Niebuhr on the predominance of the sectarian mentality in American religion. Niebuhr claims that there are no pure Churches, in the European sense, in North America, since none of these bodies attempts to become coextensive with a given area, to include the entire population of a region, and to create its own proper culture. In the eyes of Niebuhr even the traditional Churches, the Lutheran, Presbyterian, and Episcopalian, have inherited from the sects a certain bias against theology, liturgy, and hierarchical order. These Churches are influenced by the anti-intellectualism which is so characteristic of sectarian Christianity. The Churches in Canada and the United States do not readily enter into the intellectual life of the nation, establish themselves at universities, or make their contribution to the cultural and philosophical problems of the day.

The difference between Church and sect and the predominance of the sectarian spirit on this continent are of greatest importance, I believe, for the understanding of our own North American Catholicism. I believe that the weaknesses of American Catholicism are partly due to the sectarian spirit. Where are the roots of our anti-intellectualism, of our indifference to the arts, our resistance to the liturgy, and our preference for sentimental hymns and devotions? All these phenomena are certainly most foreign to Roman Catholicism. Where have we learned to build walls around ourselves, to withdraw from society, and to bypass the intellectual problems of our own generation? Why do we emphasize so much that we are different from others, and at the same time are indifferent to the richness of our own tradition? Why do we assert that we have all the truth and at the same time have no particular interest in theology? I believe that we have here, in part at least, an influence of sectarian Christianity. Usually, Catholic conservatism is aristocratic, learned, intellectual, forever listening to the great men of the past. Our own Catholic conservatism, however, is curiously hostile to history: a typical sectarian phenomenon. To this we must add the curious place which not-eating-meat-on-Friday has assumed in the psychology of American Catholics. Though the spirit of obedience is here most praiseworthy, the importance given to the practice is a phenomenon which reminds us of the sectarian attachment to special foods and particular customs. In a recent address at Washington, D.C. (which was considered important enough to be printed in the Congressional Record, 87th Congress, First Session), Reinhold Niebuhr publicly proclaimed that "even the Catholic Church becomes a sect in America—that is, not in their esteem but in our esteem." The great theologian was not offering an unkind criticism, but the perceptive judgment of an outsider. We know of course that the Catholic Church, as we recognize her with the eyes of faith, is the unique bride of Jesus Christ, the earthly body of the Lord, destined to embrace all of humanity, and hence in no way touched by the sectarian spirit. Yet we have no reason whatever to believe that this dispenses us from self-criticism and the everlasting endeavor to become more faithful to our own Catholic heritage.

These four areas or currents, then—classical Protestantism, the Anglican way, liberal religion, and the sects—constitute the frame of reference necessary to understand the Protestantism that surrounds us. These areas do not exist in strict isolation; they overlap, they influence one another, they cut across the confessional lines. But unless we understand the diversity of the forces at work, and the tremendous differences of inspiration, we cannot really understand the good and evil in Protestantism or have an intelligent ecumenical approach toward them.

From the preceding pages it is apparent that the Christian substance of these four areas must be evaluated separately. Classical Protestantism and Anglicanism have preserved a considerable attachment to the Christian past. They are loyal to traditional Christianity, they have retained important elements of the credal and sacramental life of the Christian community. Christian thinkers belonging to these two areas are constantly seeking a deeper understanding of divine revelation in the Scriptures, and a more coherent view of the world and humanity in the light of this revelation. They have produced a wealth of theological thought which is often perceptive and extremely interesting, even when we cannot agree with it. With these Christians theological dialogue is possible—and has been fruitfully going on for over a generation.

Sectarians and liberals are Christians of a different kind altogether. While the sects are attached to the ancient creeds and to the supernatural, they have reacted so violently against the rational and social elements in Christianity that they are incurably hostile to all that is ecclesiastical and theological. Since they tend to belittle reason and abstain from scholarship, it is impossible to carry on fruitful conversation with them. Most sects have not joined the World Council of Churches: they mistrust it. They are usually quite ardent enemies of the Catholic Church. Liberal Christians, on the other hand, make very good neighbors. It is easy to collaborate with them in political and cultural life. But since they reject the gratuitous, supernatural intervention of God in Jesus Christ, and the establishment of a superior order of wisdom and life over and above the realm of nature, they are not Christians at all in the traditional sense of the term. They may be baptized, but since they do not believe in Jesus Christ, true God and true man, the second Person of the Blessed Trinity who took on human flesh from the Blessed Virgin Mary, they have no conscious share in the life which the Lord has brought. Discussion with liberals on purely scholarly grounds may be rewarding, but there is no room for truly ecumenical dialogue with them. Yet this does not permit the Catholic theologian to neglect their more significant writers and to disregard intelligent and penetrating studies of religious phenomena.

We cannot close these remarks on the currents of present-day

Protestantism without mentioning, as a fifth trend, the Protestant ecumenical movement. The roots of this powerful movement are in the last century and come especially from Anglicanism and liberal Christianity. Anglicanism, due to the presence of several traditions within its own community, believed itself to be a pattern according to which religious unity could be achieved, and liberal Christians felt the tremendous urge to transform society through the service and example inspired by the gospel. The Faith and Order movement, concerned with questions of doctrine and sacraments, was largely of Anglican inspiration, at least at first, and the parallel Life and Work movement embodied the social aspirations of the liberals in the Anglo-Saxon world and, a little later, of continental Protestants.

The coming together of these two trends in the World Council of Churches produced a powerful movement to which all Protestant traditions have made an active contribution. Protestant ecumenism has produced its own proper attitudes and a new theological approach. Since the ecumenical movement strives for Christian unity, it has a deep concern for all that is Christian, present and past, and hence it is constantly confronted with ancient Christian tradition. This return to the creeds of the past and the sacramental orders of the early Church has brought about the active participation in the ecumenical movement of all Protestant (and many Orthodox) Churches and exerted an influence on large groups of liberal Christians, converting them to an orthodox faith in Christ, Lord and Savior. The vitality of the neo-orthodox revival and the serious attention given to biblical theology have profoundly influenced the World Council of Churches. Many of the Churches in the Anglo-Saxon world, which had sailed in the shallow waters of religious liberalism, have been considerably shaken, to say the least, by the biblical vision of man and the universe and the relevant witness to the redemption in Christ which they encountered in the ecumenical movement.

Since traditional Christianity is so powerful in grace, and since its analysis of the human situation is so true, we predict that the influence of the World Council of Churches will grow in the Protestant world, unless sectarian isolationism erects political obstacles for it. From the viewpoint of a Roman Catholic, the growing influence of the World Council of Churches is to be applauded. For us, the return of millions of Christians to a living faith in Christ and the kingdom he has established is a cause of great joy.

8

ECUMENISM
AND CONVERSION WORK

UNTIL NOW we have not defined Catholic ecumenism. In a general way we have regarded ecumenism as a movement in the Christian world, and in the Catholic Church, seeking the unity of all Christians through prayer, charity, co-operation, and dialogue in faith. We have seen that through the ecumenical movement Protestant Christianity has tended to move in the direction of orthodoxy, and Roman Catholics have gained a more balanced possession of Catholic fullness. The main activity of each Church remains within itself, for the people it desires principally to influence are its own members. We cannot directly change others; we can only change ourselves. How then shall we define Catholic ecumenism? Shall we conceive of it simply as a movement for Christian unity whose aim is to influence separated Christians and draw them into reconciliation with the Catholic Church, or shall we, rather, define it as a movement within the Catholic Church, perfecting the Church in a special way, bringing out the Church's latent universality, and intensifying the unity of all its members? We shall choose the second alternative. But before elaborating such a definition, we must discuss a number of serious problems raised by ecumenism in the Church.

We know from experience that ecumenism is not the only

approach to separated Christians. There exists a movement much stronger in certain countries—striving for the conversion of separated Christians to the Catholic Church. Many Catholics regard the Church's approach to separated Christians simply as part of her missionary activity to convert the world. Unbelievers must be converted to the wisdom of the gospel, and dissident Christians to the fullness of wisdom in the Church. Can this approach, called convert-making, be reconciled with the ecumenical movement?

The question is a serious one. We must note that the literature desiring to convert Protestants is usually written in an apologetical spirit: it seeks to point to the weaknesses of the Protestant position and to defend the superior claims of Catholic truth. In order to convince more readily, this kind of literature is willing to understand Protestantism through its weakest elements and to produce an abundance of arguments for the Catholic Church, even when this means oversimplification and neglect of the real problems. The tracts of convert-makers often willingly sacrifice depth to greater polemical impact.

Is this spirit reconcilable with ecumenism? We seem to face a real dilemma here. We believe that the Catholic Church is the one, true Church of Jesus Christ and no one can be saved who knowingly refuses to belong to her. This is true for the unbeliever, and this is true for every single separated Christian. Even if we believe that Christian unity is a slow historical process and that the Catholic Church in which all Christians may one day be united will differ in many ways from the present-day Church with which it is essentially identical, we believe equally that a man who recognizes the full economy of grace in regard to the Church must be willing to join her. The theological basis of conversion work is so strong that some Catholics have questioned the justification of an ecumenical movement in the Catholic Church. Fortunately, since the foundation of the Secretariat for Promoting Christian Unity, at Rome, the Catholic ecumenist need no longer defend his position. Ecumenism has become an approved movement in the Catholic Church. But this does not dispense us from trying to solve the apparent contradiction between convert-making and fruitful dialogue.

We must realize, of course, that a similar conflict also exists within Protestant Christianity. On the one hand, the Protestant ecumenical movement is concerned with peaceful dialogue and negotiations among the Churches; on the other, the conscience of the individual is regarded as supreme and, hence, may oblige a man to leave one Church to join another. In the Protestant ecumenical circles surrounding the World Council of Churches, there was a certain ethical code, unwritten and never clearly formulated, according to which the change of Church allegiance was an act of disloyalty. It was considered disloyal, not so much to the Church which one left but, rather, to the entire ecumenical movement seeking to overcome the disunity of Christians. Such a conversion, it was often felt, bypassed the real problems of the Christian world and made no contribution to Christian unity. The activity of one Church to attract and convert members of another was regarded with disfavor. Often it was called proselytism, and in ecumenical circles proselytism became a bad word.

The conflict between ecumenism and proselytism has assumed anguished proportions in recent years, when the amalgamation of the International Missionary Council with the World Council of Churches was discussed in assemblies and ecumenical literature. It was especially the Orthodox Churches, members of the World Council—though in an altogether unique fashion—who objected most vehemently to this proposal. They claimed that in certain areas Protestant missionaries try to convert Orthodox Christians to their own communities, thus upsetting the peace in the Orthodox Church; and they feared that through the integration of the International Missionary Council into the World Council these missionaries would become more powerful and continue their proselytizing among the Orthodox with added vigor and superior approval. By belonging to the World Council of Churches the Orthodox Churches would then be supporting a proselytizing movement in their own ranks.

This protest brought up the whole question of religious toleration and the right to announce the gospel according to the understanding of one's Church. The Council could not avoid studying the complex problem of religious liberty and Christian witness. The results of the study are of great interest to us, since the problems raised and some of the solutions proposed also fit into a Catholic context.

The Protestant ecumenical community is an outspoken champion of religious liberty. They believe that a man has the right to determine his relationship to God according to his conscience and that this right corresponds to the vision of man contained in the gospel.

The majority of Catholic writers of our day agree with such a biblical notion of religious liberty. It was, curiously enough, the World Council of Churches which produced a little study called *Roman Catholicism and Religious Liberty,* in which the entire Catholic literature on the subject is examined and the remarkable conclusion reached that the overwhelming majority of contemporary Catholic authors regard religious liberty as a holy gift of God. God has created man to seek his salvation in freedom, and the very gift of faith by which this salvation comes to him demands freedom of conscience. To use force or pressure of any kind in matters of faith would be against the nature of Christianity.

Though this theological viewpoint has not been accepted by the Church as the only legitimate one, there are signs that the dogmatic development in the Church points in this direction and that one day it may become the subject of a solemn declaration. The author of *Roman Catholicism and Religious Liberty* concludes his examination with this remark: "In view of the above comparison of Roman Catholic and of [Protestant] ecumenical statements on religious liberty, we think that, generally speaking, the *doctrinal* accord between ecumenism and this stream of Roman Catholic thought on the matter is highly satisfactory."

The Catholic reader must realize that this plea for religious liberty is not based on a rationalistic anthropology. The Christian arguments for religious toleration are not those proposed by the philosophers of the Enlightenment. Our arguments for religious liberty are based on the nature of man as announced in the Bible and the character of Christian faith proclaimed in the gospel. The foundation of religious liberty is supernatural. These arguments cannot be invalidated by the older approach of Catholic writers according to which truth has all the rights and error none, and consequently, erroneous religions should not be tolerated in an ideal political situation. While we agree that error has certainly no rights before God, we believe that the person erring in religion has many rights before the human community and the Christian Church. The erring person outside the Church must be treated in such a way that his Christian conscience remains free to follow the holy destiny God has bestowed on him.

Does the notion of religious liberty include the right to preach and propagate one's religion? It is one thing to be loyal to one's religious convictions and another to preach them publicly, to hold meetings of common worship, and to persuade others to join one's own community. Must we claim freedom for this kind of missionary action? The question is a delicate one. It arises among Protestants as well as Catholics, and Catholics are conscious of it with particular acuteness. We know that many "Catholic" countries have denied this freedom to Protestant groups: at the same time we have always demanded this kind of freedom for ourselves in countries which are traditionally Protestant. Will we solve this problem by proposing a double standard of morality, one for Catholic countries because Catholicism is the truth and one for Protestant countries because Protestantism is in error? But let us see first how the Protestant ecumenical community tries to solve this delicate question.

The World Council of Churches has made a unanimous declaration in favor of religious liberty and the freedom to give public witness. According to the World Council, it is wrong for a Church, and against the nature of Christianity, to use political means, pressure, or direct legislation to forbid the public worship and the missionary activity of other Christian groups. This position, we must mention, is not traditionally associated with any of the Churches, Protestant or Catholic. At one time all the Churches employed the power of the State to suppress other Christian groups. The greater freedom of religion found in the modern state is not so much the product of the Christian conscience as the result of liberal and humanistic generosity. The arguments for the freedom to give witness proposed by the World Council of Churches, however, are not based on liberal ideals but on the teaching of the gospel.

According to the Scriptures, faith in the divine acts of salvation must always be declared in public. In the Old Testament, the faith of the people in the divine covenant was constantly announced by them and to them through liturgical celebrations, the reading of the Law, and prophetical preaching. The people were regarded as God's witnesses among the nations. In the New Testament the obligation to announce the faith took on a new urgency. Since the new covenant was universal, Christianity was essentially a missionary movement, and to declare faith in Christ publicly and persuasively belonged to the very nature of the act of faith. Jesus declared, "Everyone who acknowledges me before men, I also will acknowledge him before my Father in heaven. But whoever disowns me before men, I in turn will disown him before my Father in heaven" (Matt 10:32–33). The apostles and, with them, all Christians were sent to announce the faith to the world, even when this meant suffering and persecution. The believer in the New Testament is necessarily one who gives witness. The freedom a man needs to believe in the Christian message must be accompanied by the freedom to profess it publicly. These freedoms cannot be separated; they belong together. In the eyes of the World Council of Churches, therefore, it is the God-given right of any man to make his Christian commitment according to his own conscience, and to announce it publicly for others to hear and to follow.

On the other hand, the World Council of Churches is realistic enough to realize that the freedom of missionary activity must be defined more carefully. It cannot mean that Christian missionaries or sectarian groups have the right to disturb the peace of a Christian community and upset simple people by preaching new doctrines. It was precisely to prevent proselytism that the World Council undertook this study of religious liberty and Christian witness. The member Churches of the Council wanted some guarantee that the amalgamation of the Missionary Council and the World Council would not encourage missionary movements to convert their own members.

To solve the problem, the study commission of the World Council introduced an important distinction which, as far as I know, had never been made before. The official report distinguishes between authentic Christian witness on the one hand, and the corruption of this witness on the other. The corruption of witness is called proselytism. Since the description of this proselytism is of greatest significance also from a Catholic viewpoint, we must look at the whole passage referring to it:

Witness is corrupted when cajolery, bribery, undue pressure or intimidation is used—subtly or openly—to bring about seeming conversion; when we put the success of one Church before the honour of Christ; when we commit the dishonesty of comparing the ideal of our own Church with the actual achievement of another; when we seek to advance our own cause by bearing false witness against another Church; when personal or corporate self-seeking replaces love for every individual soul with whom we are concerned. Such corruption of the Christian witness indicates lack of confidence in the power of the Holy Spirit, lack of respect for the nature of man and lack of recognition of the true character of the gospel. It is very easy to recognize these faults and sins in others; it is necessary to acknowledge that we are all liable to fall into one or the other of them ourselves.

Proselytism is here defined as the use of unfair means in the proclamation of the gospel. To this no man and no institution have a right. In the eyes of the World Council of Churches this is the theological principle limiting the freedom of Christians in their public testimonies. According to the Council, Christians have the right and the duty to give witness to their faith, even when they do it among members of other Churches; but this witness must remain pure and authentic, and must not deviate in the various ways described above. These are severe strictures. Though the World Council takes a stand on religious freedom to believe and to preach one's Christian convictions, it does subject all missionary activity to a strict ethical code.

It is not surprising that many sectarian groups and smaller missionary societies are displeased with the attitude of the World Council of Churches. Some of the evangelical groups have always been hostile to the World Council and to the International Missionary Council associated with it. It is interesting to note that the majority of Protestant missionaries actively engaged in South America belong to sectarian groups opposed to the ecumenical movement. When the plans for the fusion of the two large Councils were discussed, several smaller missionary societies belonging to the International Missionary Council withdrew their membership. They did not, seemingly, want to accept the limitation of their activity by the standards of ecumenical charity.

We now understand the lines along which the Protestant ecumenical community seeks to solve the conflict between ecumenical dialogue and the search for individual conversions. Today both movements are regarded as legitimate, necessary, and demanded by the present situation of Christianity. Ecumenism is necessary because our common guilt has divided us and therefore marred the gift of Christ, and, conversely, giving witness for the sake of the conversion of others is necessary, since the gospel itself demands it from us. If the faith of Christians includes a definite creed regarding the true nature of the Church, then they are obliged to announce this faith to Christians separated from them. This activity, according to the World Council of Churches, does not create a conflict with ecumenism as long as the Christian witness is inspired by truthfulness, charity, humility, and respect.

Will the Orthodox Church, frightened by Protestant missionaries among their people, be satisfied with this solution? Ideally, it may well be that they will. If people are well trained in the teachings and the sacramental life of their Church, they are not likely easily to be swayed by the sermon of a Protestant preacher who remains within the limits imposed by ecumenical charity. How highly de we treasure supernatural truth if we believe that another doctrine can easily replace it? In reality, however, an Orthodox community may consist of men who are neither well instructed in their religion nor fervent in their practice of the liturgy; in this case, the simple words of a less complex creed may well sound overly attractive. Here a Protestant sermon may cause trouble in the community. But what is the situation then? According to the ecumenical ideal of the World Council, Orthodox Christians should regard the Protestant minister as a challenge, making them more devoted to the instruction of their people and more eager to lead them to a vital sacramental life.

What is the Catholic position on these difficult matters? As Catholics, we are in the unique situation—along with the Orthodox—of believing that the gospel of Christ contains a definite message of the Church. We believe that the Catholic Church with its center at Rome is the earthly body of the Lord, the bride of Christ, the holy Church of God. We believe, therefore, that any man who understands the full truth of the gospel, whether he is far away from us in atheism or near to us as a baptized believer, must join the Catholic Church to find his salvation, and that to fall away from this Catholic Church by an act of apostasy is to exclude oneself from Christ and life everlasting.

At the same time, the ecumenical dialogue is an accepted movement within the Catholic Church. We have shown, moreover, that the Catholic view, or a Catholic view, of religious freedom is in substantial conformity with that of the World Council of Churches.

We must also insist that the Catholic tradition has always held that the act of faith implies and includes public witness. A reliable testimony to this view is the *Summa* of St. Thomas, in which the interior act of faith is considered essentially one with the public confession (II–II, 3, 1). Faith in the heart and faith on the lips are one and the same before God. Either Christian faith is announced before men, or it is not faith at all. From this it follows that, from the Catholic viewpoint, a separated Christian possessing the virtue of faith is by this very gift obliged, despite his objective errors, to profess his faith in public, to worship God in the community, and to announce his creed so that others may follow it. From the Catholic viewpoint, the Protestant Christian in good faith would sin if he failed to give witness. Despite the errors mixed in his creed, he is objectively obliged to testify to his commitment to Christ. We must conclude, therefore, that if we advocate religious liberty on the biblical arguments proposed above, we must also defend the liberty to announce one's Christian convictions publicly and to seek the conversions of others. A prophetical religion is essentially missionary.

The Catholic will be grateful to the study commission of the World Council for the excellent report on proselytism. We agree wholeheartedly with the distinction between authentic witness and the corruption of witness, even if we do not describe it in precisely the same terms. The use of unfair means in the proclamation of the gospel is a constant temptation. If all Christians, including ourselves, were to take this distinction seriously, in other words, if all of us were to fight this temptation as a great evil, ecumenism and evangelization would not be in conflict. We would be saved from the hateful and untruthful propaganda spread against us by uneducated and unkind sectarians. From the authentic witness of Protestants we have nothing to fear. And if we ourselves become truthful, charitable, and humble in announcing the Catholic gospel among dissident Christians, our apostolate of individual conversions will not contradict or even harm the Catholic ecumenical movement, or be disloyal to the ideals of the Protestant ecumenical community.

It is well known that in reality there is much friction between the Churches. In areas where the Catholic Church is intransigent, Protestants are usually aggressive and insulting, and hence each side is prevented from correcting itself by the faults present in the other. It is my conviction, however, that the true Church of Christ should be the first to follow the gospel spirit, even if this increases, for a time, the attacks of hostile men against her. We must have faith. Ultimately, evil men are helpless in their desire to harm the Church. We must believe that the fate of the Church is in the keeping of the Holy Ghost.

In this chapter we defend the view that both ecumenism and the apostolate of conversions are legitimate in the Catholic Church, and that in this we do not contradict the ideals of the World Council of Churches. Since ecumenism is fairly new in the Catholic Church, many Catholics and non-Catholics believe that convert-making corresponds to a deeper desire of the Church. Many feel that ecumenism is a concession of the Church, seeing that other Christians will not be converted, or that it is a roundabout way of converting others while they are not watching.

It must be observed, however, that the Catholic Church, when faced with bodies of separated Christians, has always preferred to deal with the problem collectively. This is most obvious in regard to the separated Eastern Churches, where Rome has never permitted any kind of conversion work. The positive acts of the Holy See have always been negotiations with the patriarchs and bishops of the Eastern Churches in the hope of preparing an ecclesiastical reconciliation. In certain areas where Orthodox and Catholic Christians mingled, or where Orthodox immigrants were isolated from their own Churches, Catholics may have attempted to draw them into their own Church. Without necessarily approving the methods that have been used in these cases, the undertaking seems to me quite legitimate. Many Orthodox Christians, isolated from their Churches either by distance or by the new culture they acquired, were in need of the support of brethren and the sacramental worship of the Church. It would be most unfortunate to see them lose their ancient Christian heritage by joining a new Protestant group, and hence to point out to them the closeness of Catholicism to their own religious tradition is surely a holy undertaking which is not disloyal to the larger ecumenical quest between the Churches.

Even in regard to Protestants, the first attempt of the Catholic Church to overcome the unholy cleavage was directed to Protestants collectively, not through the conversion of individuals. Though we are not proud to recall the past, we must remember that it was mainly by political power and advantageous treaties that the Roman Church sought to regain many of the territories which had fallen away. This was certainly no ecumenical movement, but it does show that the Catholic Church realized that the tremendous evil of separation could never be healed by the conversion of individuals. If there is a solution, it must affect groups of peoples, whole Churches, cultural areas, Christian communities.

Even today this seems to me the only sound position. However important the apostolate of conversions may be in certain situations, it is not the Church's response to the divided state of Christianity. Conversion work by itself bypasses the real problems of Christian disunity, the purification of the dissident Christian traditions, and the transformation of the Church herself toward greater catholicity.

On the other hand, we admit that the ecumenical movement we have described in these pages is not equally important in all areas where Catholics and Protestants live together. One might propose the principle that the closer a Christian Church is to the fullness of the Catholic tradition, the more important is ecumenical work and the less significant the work for individual conversions; and, conversely, that the further a Christian group is from this Catholic fullness, the less significant is ecumenism and the more important the apostolate for individual souls. This law is actually verified by the attitude of the Catholic Church in various areas of the world. In regard to the Eastern Churches, as we have mentioned, the only legitimate method is that of ecumenism. In regard to Protestant Christians, Catholic ecumenism is fully developed in the countries of Europe where the Catholic Church faces a fairly homogeneous community of Protestants committed to a traditional creed, a liturgy, and a common theological tradition. It is not surprising, therefore, that in English-speaking countries Catholic ecumenism has not had the same evolution; here the Catholic Church faces a great variety of Protestant traditions, many of them quite distant from traditional Christianity. The reason why Catholics in these countries have remained so little impressed by ecumenism and why they have sometimes even resented it, lies, in part, in the particular kind of Protestantism which they encounter. The radical reaction against liberalism which a generation ago transformed the Protestantism of continental Europe did not achieve the same effect in England and North America. Since liberalism as well as sectarianism abounds in the English-speaking Christian world, many

Catholics have not been sensitive to the authentic Christian forces among their Protestant neighbors.

Especially in North America there are vast numbers of men who call themselves Christian and Protestant without any truly religious commitment to the God of Jesus Christ. They do not know the teaching of Scriptures, and they do not believe in the central message of the Gospel: the Incarnation and the Trinity. For many of them God is a friendly being full of benevolence for nice people; he also has a predilection for democracy. The gospel is a charter of the good neighbor policy and economic freedom. These people are usually loyal to their Churches. In fact, going to church on Sundays has become a public pledge that one respects the domesticated values of the benevolent God in favor of democratic ideals and free enterprise. These "Protestants" have no other connection with the authentic Protestantism of the Reformation than the weekly offering they make to their Churches. Faced with people of this kind, the Catholic Church has only one answer: To give witness to the Catholic gospel in order that those whom God chooses may find the new life of Christ in the Church of his founding. While it is imperative that the Catholic community become more imbued with the ecumenical spirit—for the sake of its own inner renewal—it is also indispensable that the Church continue her effort to convert individuals. There need be no conflict here. Ecumenism makes the Church more truly Catholic, and conversion work deals with individual souls whose religious convictions are only vaguely related to traditional Christianity.

We have mentioned that the apostolate for conversions is reconcilable with ecumenism and Christian charity only when it is subject to a high ethical code. We must discuss this topic in greater detail.

We support the distinction introduced by the World Council

of Churches between authentic Christian witness and the corruption of this witness, though we cannot agree with the rigid terms of the distinction. There is no witness which is perfectly pure! As long as we are in this world, Christian missionary activity will always be influenced by a certain number of selfish desires. It would be hypocritical to reject altogether the value of Christian witness whenever we detect in it some measure of self-seeking. The imperfect motive weakens but does not invalidate the good deed. It is true that Christian witness depends much more than any other activity on the purity of intention, since the effect of missionary witness is completely dependent on God's mercy; yet, even here, the partial egotism involved in it does not entirely corrupt the witness.

The report of the World Council of Churches mentions four distinct faults by which the movement of evangelization deteriorates and becomes proselytism. The first fault mentioned is the use of bribes, intimidations, and force in the propagation of the gospel. These means are obviously wrong, and even though we have often used them in the past, everyone agrees that they are reprehensible and against the gospel. The people who made use of such means have usually done so with a bad conscience, for they knew that God cannot be served by evil ways.

The second fault is the preference of particular ecclesiastical advantages to the good of the people or the hidden action of Jesus Christ. This is a more subtle temptation, and we may fall into it unawares. There are situations where, for the sake of financial support for schools or some other ecclesiastical benefit, the bishops of a country favor a political party or a particular politician whose ideals are at variance with social justice or Christian freedom. Catholic political notions do not exclude a state which protects and supports the Church, but this is precisely the reason why we are so often tempted to exploit a political situation in an unfair way against those who disagree with us spiritually. If the propagation of faith goes hand in hand with such methods, we sin and our Christian witness is greatly weakened.

The third fault mentioned in the report is the giving of false witness in regard to other Churches. In order to protect our own people against the influence of others, we are tempted to paint their beliefs and practices in dark colors, to misrepresent their teachings, and to slander their good intentions. To increase the persuasive power of our arguments for the Catholic Church, we may be tempted to belittle or even deny the authentic Christian elements and sacramental realities in dissident religious groups. Following such a method, we might convert dissident Christians to the Catholic Church by neglecting, instead of perfecting, their own Christian heritage; this would be reprehensible proselytism. A particularly subtle way of being unfair would be to draw a comparison between the *ideal* state of the Catholic Church and the *actual* achievements of other Christian bodies. We might describe the Church's unity, her catholicity and sanctity in the normative terms of our faith, and then compare these with the actual situation found in other Churches, including their shortcomings and faulty developments. This is obviously unjust. As Father Dumont has said so well, when we try to understand Protestant Christians, we must not only look at what they are but also at what they want to be.

A fourth fault which may weaken authentic Christian witness is to let group egotism, instead of concern for souls, dominate our missionary zeal. We may be tempted to convert others for our own glory rather than for the good of their souls. Our personal selfishness is easily projected and extended to the group with which we identify ourselves. Corporate self-seeking is a phenomenon found in all families, peoples, and religious communities. There is no promise in revelation that the Holy Spirit, living in the Church, will remove all symptoms of group egotism from our midst. It is, unfortunately, possible to love the Church from the impulse of our wounded nature; it is possible to fight for the Church, to defend her, to give all one's energy to her service without supernatural inspiration. Our fervor might be a prolongation of our selfishness. We might fight for her in order to enjoy our triumph over others; we might defend her in order to revel in our own infallibility; we might labor for her glory in order to be successful and appreciated in this world. If a missionary activity or any form of the apostolate is inspired by egotistical impulses and therefore neglects the true good of souls, our witness to Christ is greatly weakened and we raise obstacles to the spread of the kingdom among men.

The moral principles we have mentioned are immediately convincing. It is curious that they have never been discussed in our moral theology. There exists no study on the moral aspects of missionary activity, of apologetics, and of the work for individual conversions. Here again the ecumenical movement leads us to a greater fidelity to the Word of God.

There need be, then, no conflict between ecumenism and conversion work, whether it is carried on by Protestants or Catholics. It is my conviction that the Catholic work for individual conversions will become more truly effective when it is deeply influenced by the ecumenism of the Church.

A priest whose theological training has been carried on in an ecumenical spirit will find it much easier to express Catholic doctrines in the language of others; he will be able to translate our traditional terms and show how they are relevant to the contemporary world. More than that, he will appreciate the good he finds in others. Too often, the priest dedicated to convert-making presents the Catholic truth as something altogether new, having no direct link with the Christian convictions of others, instead of trying to present Catholic teaching as the fulfillment of their Christian aspirations. If a man has Christian faith, entry into the Catholic Church is not a radical break with his past (like the conversion of a nonbeliever), but a fulfillment and a completion. Too often converts are drawn into the form of Catholicism which happens to surround them, instead of being encouraged to find the kind of spirituality in the Church which is in harmony with their own background and their deep aspirations. Local customs and the ideals of one kind of piety are often presented to him as belonging to the substance of Catholicism.

The new convert is often overwhelmed by what appears to him to be, but is not, ecclesiastical authority. As a result, the unfolding of his creative and spiritual powers promised to him in the Church never really takes place. He will often simply follow the convictions that surround him, without ever having any new ideas or taking any original action himself. Because of the break that has been created in his life, before and after his conversion, because of the effort completely to revise his intellectual life, he no longer finds the right words for communicating with his family and his former friends. He becomes isolated from them, not because they reject him, but because he has been led to give up the continuity with his life before he was converted. If convert instruction were given in an ecumenical spirit, the converts would become bridges and links to their former communities. Separated Christians would be able to see the convert as one of their own, as one who has remained loyal to their Christian ideals and yet as one who has received an immensely richer treasure in the Catholic Church.

The famous converts from Protestantism may be divided into two groups. There are those who, rejecting their past completely, seek in the Catholic Church the spirituality most opposed to their old outlook. And there are others who, cherishing their past as a stage on the road to Catholic fullness, seek in the Catholic Church a spirituality in continuity with their former Christian ideals. F. W. Faber belonged to the first group, and Cardinal Newman, who never saw eye to eye with him, to the second. The Fabers of history have harmed the ecumenical movement, the Newmans have aided it. Gertrude von Le Fort, the great German poetess, convert from Protestant Christianity, has observed that there are converts who anticipate and experience in their hearts the true reconciliation of Protestants with the Catholic Church.

After having described Catholic ecumenism in various ways and contrasted it with the apostolate for souls, we wish to define its essential features. There are many reasons why we prefer to define the Catholic ecumenical movement, not in relation to dissident Christians, but in relation to the Church herself. In this way we make clear that the movement is profoundly Catholic and distinguish it more sharply from conversion work and direct influence on dissident Christians. The ecumenical dialogue certainly influences separated Christians, but this effect is incidental. It will have this influence precisely because we do not seek it. We must characterize the Catholic striving after Christian unity in a way which makes very clear that the ecumenical movement is not a cunning technique for making converts. We shall regard Catholic ecumenism as an activity seeking to perfect the Church in one of her essential qualities. What is this quality?

By the catholicity of the Church theological writers usually understand the universality of the Church in regard to place and people. The Church is sent and established as the unique community of salvation embracing all of humanity, and hence she is not bound to any particular people, to any race or country, to any cultural or social class. This radical universality belongs to the Church because of what Christ has done for her. He is the universal Savior. The missionary activity of the Catholic Church tries to translate this gift into the concrete order of history. When theologians write of the qualitative catholicity of the Church, they do not refer to her geographical extension, but to the universal character of the message of Christ and the life of the Church, which are capable of adaptation to the mentality of every people, to the genius of every culture, and the talents of any human community.

This qualitative catholicity has been greatly emphasized by

the recent pontiffs in their encyclicals on the missions and in some documents on the Christian situation in Europe. In the encyclical letter of 1937, *Mit brennender Sorge,* Pius XI stated:

Under the enormous vault of the Church there is room for the development of the special qualities, talents, tasks, and vocations which God the Creator and Redeemer has bestowed on individuals and on whole nations. The maternal heart of the Church is great and wide enough to see in the development, according to God's plan, of such proper qualities and special talents, the richness of variety rather than the danger of isolation.

Pius XII, emphasizing the Church's universality, wrote in the encyclical *Summi Pontificatus:*

Those who enter the Church, whatever their origin or their speech, must know that they have equal rights in the house of the Lord where the law of Christ and the peace of Christ prevail.

This catholicity possesses a special factor dealing with the properly ecclesiastical domain. The Church's catholicity is such that she is not bound to any particular rite, a unique liturgy, a single school of theology, or any one ascetical tradition. "The Church is not Latin," Benedict XV wrote, "neither is she Greek or Slavonic, but Catholic." The Church is fully catholic or, to signify the special ecclesiastical factor of catholicity, the Church is fully *ecumenical* because she can integrate into her own life a plurality of rites, of liturgies, of theological schools, of disciplinary traditions, of ascetical practices. According to the repeated promises made by the popes to the Eastern Churches, the integration of these different values does not weaken the Church or imply compromise and inner conflict; on the contrary, they proclaim a plenitude of Christian life and a special splendor of Christ's body. We may speak of the *ecumenicity* of the Church, a note or quality within the Church's catholicity, signifying the potential plurality of ecclesiastical forms and theological traditions within the Church which bring to light the richness and universality of Christ's gift.

In his letters dealing with the Eastern Churches, Pius XI often spoke of the *ecumenical* unity of the Church. With this adjective he singled out that aspect of the Church's catholicity by which she embraces, at least potentially, all authentic Christian traditions in the freedom of a diversified unity. This ecumenical character of ecclesiastical unity was, in the eyes of Pius XI, a visible mark authenticating the Church's message. In *Ecclesiam Dei* he wrote: "The Church of God, wonderfully established as a universal family of brethren and destined to embrace the entire human race, is recognizable in the world, with other signs, through her ecumenical unity."

We therefore regard the Catholic ecumenical movement as an activity within the Church making her more ecumenical, that is, making more manifest her ecumenicity. Catholic ecumenism seeks to open the Church to the plurality of gifts promised by Christ, thus leading her away from one-sidedness in usage and the preference for one particular rite and cultural uniformity. It is clear to a Catholic that not all traditions that call themselves Christian can be integrated into the Church, but only those that are in agreement with the gospel. It is precisely the task of the ecumenical dialogue to distinguish in other Christian communities the elements that are in harmony with Catholic life and hence could be integrated, and the elements in contradiction to Catholic life, and, consequently, forever irreconcilable. The ecumenical movement renews the Church's vitality, opening new possibilities of spiritual and ecclesiastical life, adapting it to every culture and to all authentic Christian forms of expression inspired by the Holy Ghost.

This quality of ecumenicity is entirely different from what Anglicans call "comprehensiveness." Comprehensiveness is an external juxtaposition of various ecclesiastical traditions in a single body, containing elements which are not only logical contradictories, but which also reveal divergent and irreconcilable visions of the gospel. The ecumenicity of the Catholic Church, on the other hand, is the unfolding of the fullness of Christ's gift from within, as it is applied and extended to the various peoples of God's world and adapted to the different spiritual traditions of the Christian past.

On the other hand, the effectual ecumenicity of the Catholic Church cannot be taken for granted. The ecumenical ideal we have described demands sacrifices and generosity on our part. We have to discover anew the value of diversity. Since a natural tendency of the human mind seeks to identify unity and uniformity, we are tempted to think, at least occasionally, that an increasing uniformity might more convincingly express the unity of Christ's Church. In reality, however, an excessive uniformity obscures the unity which Christ has given to his people; unity is fully catholic only when we find faith, holiness, and obedience in the freedom of our personal vocation and social tradition.

In this connection, let us listen to two Cardinals of the Catholic Church expressing their ideas and hopes for future developments. Cardinal Feltin, Archbishop of Paris, says:

It is not enough for a bishop to say that since his mission is to unite, he must employ all the forces of unity and fight all the forces of division. This is much too simple a solution, for, most of the time, the forces of division are no more than the inevitable consequence of a diversity which is of such a value that it would be unfortunate to sacrifice it for unity.*

Cardinal Alfrink, Archbishop of Utrecht, expresses himself in the same way. He says:

Obviously, the Church could never accept a pluralism of truth. Truth is one. Thus the Church must give her all to protect the unity of revealed truth. On the other hand, she ought not to be afraid of

* *The Catholic Messenger* (Davenport, Iowa), January 11, 1962.

pluralism in the practice of this unique faith if, in a precise period, this pluralism can aid in laying bare the essential characteristics of the Church. It is licit to think that a certain uniformity hides the true unity of the Church from view, and that the very fact of a positive diversity in the practice of the faith can, on the contrary, make the nature of this unity stand out more effectively.*

Catholic ecumenism is an activity in the Church which makes her more universal, more Catholic, more perfect, more true to the hidden beauty Christ bestowed on her on the day of his victory on the cross.

* *The Catholic Messenger* (Davenport, Iowa), December 21, 1961.

9

CHRISTIANS AND JEWS

THE JEWS are related to the ecumenical dialogue in many ways. They do not belong to it, strictly speaking, but seeing that Christianity is rooted in the people of the Old Law, that biblical concepts and sacramental symbols come to us from the Jewish people, and that, moreover, the Church proclaims herself to be the messianic fulfillment and authentic heir of ancient Israel, the relationship between Jews and Christians is intimately connected with the ecumenical conversation between Christian Churches.

There are many reasons why Christian theologians, both Catholic and Protestant, have shown a special interest in the Jewish people and the mystery of Israel. The renewal of biblical theology has powerfully reminded us that a study of the Old Testament sheds light on the realities of the New, and that even questions such as the unity and holiness of the Church can be deepened by studying God's ways with the Israel of old. We have made some applications of these principles in the preceding chapters.

Eschatology, the branch of theology which has been given so much attention in recent decades by both Protestants and Catholics, has also brought to light the relation of the Church of Christ to the Jewish people. Since eschatology deals with the completion of Christ's redemptive work at the end of time and the meaning which this last event gives to our existence in the present, the ultimate return of the Jewish people to the community of salvation, announced in the Epistle to the Romans, has attracted the attention of theological writers. In this sense, measuring her by the prophecy as yet to be fulfilled, the Church cannot be called complete without Israel.

It was the power of modern history—an anti-Semitic outburst of gigantic proportions and the foundation of the new state of Israel—more than theological and ecclesiological interests, that has turned the eyes of the world to the Jewish people. Christian authors have approached the Church's relation to Jews with a new concern, since they have realized in our day that a consistent racial anti-Semitism will ultimately turn against Christianity. If a man despises the Jews on principle, he will eventually also despise the Jew Jesus Christ, the Son of the eternal God.

The contact between Christians and Jews today takes place in the form of dialogue. Christians have studied Jewish religion and have listened to Jewish voices, and Jews have studied Christianity and have been willing to listen to us. Though this is not an ecumenical dialogue, we believe that it contains some of the elements of ecumenical encounter. There is learning going on in this dialogue. It leads us to discover new dimensions of charity. It forces us to review our past theology and return to the more authentic positions of antiquity. It reminds us of elements of our past which we have forgotten and neglected. It removes prejudices on both sides and opens the way, not only to a better mutual understanding, but also to a more powerful divine action in our hearts. If these are characteristics of ecumenical dialogue, our conversation with Jews may, in this limited sense, be called ecumenical.

The most immediate result of this dialogue was the discovery on the part of Christians that a certain way of preaching the gospel, and certain theological theories passed on in their writings, have been contributing factors, at least remote ones, to the anti-Jewish feeling so widespread in the Christian world. Re-reading the Christian authors from the fourth century on through the Middle Ages almost to modern times, we find that the proclamation of the gospel was often, though not always, surrounded by legends regarding the Jews. Often they were depicted as a perfidious, stiff-necked people. Often they were represented as an accursed people, condemned for the crucifixion of Jesus, reaping their just punishment in this world. Many Christian scholars, having been forced to it by their Jewish partners, have examined the Christian documents of the past; their findings are devastating. So terrible is the record of anti-Jewish preaching that many Christian authors today hesitate to speak of the Christian "mission" to the Jews. They are too embarrassed.

In a more positive way, the dialogue between Christians and Jews has forced Christian theologians to elaborate a theology of Israel and to lay down the principles of the Christian approach to the Jews. The literature which has been produced is very large, even though not much of it has appeared in English.*

We believe and affirm that the divine economy of salvation is one and undivided. This is the first principle. God's self-revelation to Israel through the patriarchs and Moses was the first stage of the universal redemption revealed to all men in Jesus Christ. The two convenants, the old and the new, are not separate attempts by God to reconcile men with himself, but one single drama of redemption, beginning in Israel, confirmed by the covenant of Sinai, and endorsed, fulfilled, and elevated by the new covenant in the blood of Jesus Christ shed on Calvary. In this sense we may say with the ancient Fathers that the Church began in the Old Testament. The institutions of the old covenant announced and, to a degree, anticipated the fulfillment they prepared. In this sense Abel belonged to the Church; Abraham

---

* Among English-speaking Catholics no one has thought about these matters more than Msgr. John Oesterreicher, who has explained his doctrine to the author in many private conversations.

did; Moses and the prophets did. "Abraham rejoiced at the thought of seeing my day," Jesus said, and then added, "He did see it and was glad" (John 8:56).

The division of the one history of salvation into two periods, Christ's Advent and Christ's Presence, is traditional in the Church. It means that the God who revealed himself in the Old Testament is the same who spoke to us in the New. It means that the God of Abraham, Isaac, and Jacob is the Father of Jesus Christ. It means, moreover, that the religion of Abraham and Moses was truly divine in origin and that the same Holy Spirit who inspired the writings of the Old Testament inspired also those of the New. These are fundamental truths which are worth being clearly pronounced.

It is untrue, therefore, and against Catholic doctrine, to distinguish between the God of the Old Testament, calling him a God of wrath, and the God of the New Testament, calling him a God of love. This is not only wrong, but blasphemous. It is true that in the progressive revelation, which was God's plan for redeeming the universe, the full measure of his love was not revealed before the coming of his eternal Son in the flesh; but the covenants which God made with man prior to the final and perfect one already revealed his mercy and love for that mankind which had turned away from him. It would be equally wrong to contrast the teachings of the Old Testament with those of the New as if the one advocated revenge and justice, and the other mercy and forgiveness. While revelation was progressive, and hence the moral doctrines of the New Testament may well transcend those of the Old, God had prepared for the teaching of his Son Jesus through the insights given to his prophets and the wisdom granted to the great in Israel. The tendency, often encountered in the past, to belittle Jewish religion in order to glorify Christianity, it is not in harmony with Catholic doctrine. The apostles rejected the beliefs and the practices of Judaism, not because they were bad, but because they were only preparations for the fulfillment, and hence had become meaningless once the Savior had appeared.

Modern research has shown that many Christian books used to slander the faith of Israel and inspire a certain contempt for the Jewish people on account of their religion. We have often delighted in representing the Jewish religion at the time of Our Lord in terms of decadence and hypocrisy, basing our view exclusively on certain prophetical passages of the New Testament, thus losing the key to the true understanding of Jesus' mission. We overlooked his Jewish background, his fidelity to the Law, his temple worship, in short, his share in the faith of his own people. In the eyes of many Christians, Jesus has ceased to be the Jew he is the New Testament. We have often regarded him simply as the universal man, forgetting that he is the son of David, born of a Jewish maiden, obedient to the Law, and that if he had not been the son of Israel, the ancient promises would not yet be fulfilled and we would still be unredeemed. We must confess that in the imagination of the Christian people, Judas is more Jewish than Jesus, and the Pharisees more Jewish than Mary and the apostles. This is, of course, absurd.

This leads us to the second principle illuminating the theology of Israel. The foundation of the Church was the fulfillment of the promises made to Israel. Jesus came as the promised messias in order to redeem his people, and it was in this people that he gave his teaching and performed his redemptive action. Jesus hardly ever spoke to Gentiles in the Gospel. "I was not sent except to the lost sheep of the House of Israel" (Matt 15:24), he told the Canaanite woman who pleaded with him to help her daughter, and he answered her prayers only after seeing the extent of her confidence. The passion, death, and resurrection of Jesus, the descent of the Holy Spirit, and the entire establishment of the Christian Church took place within Israel. It is important to stress this, since we have often created the impression that the Jews have rejected Jesus and hence were disowned by him. We have often presented the story of human salvation as if the crucifixion of Jesus had excluded the Jews from the love of God, and as if the covenant with them had been dissolved and a new one made with the Gentiles. We even read the theory that the Jews have been cursed and condemned.

If we study the Scriptures carefully, however, we discover that the coming of Jesus divided the people of Israel. There were those who were for him, and those against him. The poor and humble were with the Lord; and the proud, the rich, and the powerful were largely against him. The evangelists and St. Paul teach that the promises made to Israel were indeed fulfilled within Israel, in that chosen section of the people where the words of the Lord bore fruit. This is a repetition of an Old Testament pattern: while the multitude were indifferent to the Lord and destined to be chastised, a holy remnant, elected by grace, was loyal to the covenant. The prophets had announced that even on the Day of the Lord it would be this faithful remnant that was to be saved. The early Church, made up entirely of Jews, regarded itself as this faithful remnant of Israel, purified in the blood of Christ and transformed into the universal community of salvation. It is not true to say, therefore, that the covenant has been abrogated and a new one made with another people, as if there were a discontinuity in God's plan of salvation. What happened rather was that the old covenant was fulfilled in the new. The promises came true in Israel, and the renewed and spiritualized Israel, the Church of Jerusalem, the "Israel of God" (Gal 6:16), was the stem into which the Gentiles were grafted. In this true Israel, cleansed in the blood of Christ, the Gentiles became sharers in the promises made to Abraham and in the privileges of the chosen people.

We immediately see how wrong and unbiblical are the stories told a hundred times over that the Jews were rejected because of their responsibility for the crucifixion. It is true that Jews were more guilty in this awful crime than were the Roman procurator and his soldiers; but this was so, and had to be so, because the entire work of salvation took place within the Jewish people. Jesus himself was the Jewish savior; he was accepted by some Jews—Mary, the disciples, the crowds—and rejected by others, especially Jewish officialdom. In the New Testament the Jews are symbols of the entire human race. Their acceptance of the Lord, especially that of the Blessed Virgin, represents the faith of all men; their rejection of Jesus, especially by the Jerusalem clergy, stands for the sin of all of us in resisting grace. Christianity became universal only after the glorification, when Jesus was made both Christ and Lord over Jews and Gentiles alike.

It is absurd, then, to speak of the rejection of the Jews after the crucifixion. Jesus was messias and redeemer of the Jews after his resurrection even more than before. St. Peter solemnly announced to the Jews of Jerusalem that the man Jesus, whom they had crucified, God had made both Christ and Lord for them (cf. Acts 2:36). By believing in him they had access to the kingdom. The generation who rejected the message of the Lord was to be chastised in the destruction of Jerusalem, as forewarned and foretold by the Lord; but this destruction was precisely the reverse side of Jesus' victory over sin and death, and hence another proof of Jesus' messiasship for Israel. There is no biblical reason whatever for extending the punishment of those who repudiated Christ's message further than the destruction of Jerusalem. The threats of Jesus pronounced against his city find their realization here. To speak of a further chastisement for the events leading to the crucifixion, apart from that which we all deserve—by our sins we have all become guilty of Christ's death—is to produce unjustified fables.

Since we are conscious of the enormous harm which the simple sentence "the Jews have crucified Jesus" has done in the world, we must never pronounce it without immediately adding that Jesus himself was a Jew, that all the events of our salvation took place in a Jewish setting, and that the Jewish people were divided in their reaction to the Lord.

In the light of these biblical facts, clearly expressed in the Catholic liturgy, the opinion that a divine curse rests on the Jewish people is an untrue story, a malevolent legend, which has had the saddest consequences throughout history. Too often ancient and medieval Christian sermons surrounded the Jews with sacred horror. It was then believed that, after their rejection, Jewish religion had become perverted, demoniacal, and the source of evil in the world. Even though the more gruesome legends disappeared from Christian books in modern times, the story of the malediction on the people is found in many respectable manuals, commentaries on Scripture, and popular interpretations of the Bible. For this reason, Cardinal Lienart, Bishop of Lille, dedicated his pastoral letter of Easter 1960 to the mystery of Israel. In his message he refuted the legend of "the curse" and any form of spiritual anti-Semitism. The Cardinal declared that "the religious destiny of Israel is a mystery of grace on which Christians must meditate with a respectful sympathy."*

Anti-Semitism is incompatible with Christianity. It is, first of all, contrary to the universality of redemption, as is any form of racism. The hatred of any ethnic group or human family cannot go hand in hand with faith in Christ. The catholicity of love is the touchstone of Christianity. "If anyone says 'I love God' and hates his brother, he is a liar" (1 John 4:20). Hatred for the Jewish people, however, has an added vice in it, for if a man detests all Jews he will also detest the Jew Jesus Christ, or at least regret that the eternal God has become man as a son of the Jewish people.

There is still a third principle, derived from Scripture, which illumines the mystery of Israel. In the Epistle to the Romans, Paul tells us that God has fulfilled his promises to Israel *once* in the holy remnant, in the Jews who believed in Christ, and that

---

* See Appendix 2 for the text of Cardinal Lienart's pastoral letter.

he will fulfill his promises again in the other part of Israel, in those who now refuse to believe. By their unbelief the Jews cut themselves off from the community of salvation; as a group, they are now outside. But they will not lose their identity among the nations. The care of God's first love will accompany them; and at the moment of God's choosing, they shall return to the kingdom of Christ. St. Paul announces: "Blindness has fallen upon a part of Israel, but only until the tale of the Gentile nations is complete; then the whole of Israel will find salvation" (Rom 11:25). The apostle proclaims the hope that after the full number of the Gentiles have entered the Church, the unbelieving section of Israel will also return to the kingdom of their messias.

St. Paul does not give us any details as to when and how the reconciliation of the Jews is to take place. He refers to it several times in symbolic language—he writes, for instance, that "their reception [into the kingdom] will be life from the dead" (Rom 11:15)—but it is not given to him to say more than that the return of the unbelieving Israel will be a decisive event in the history of salvation. While the Catholic tradition, the Fathers of antiquity, and the medieval theologians are unanimous in teaching the final reconciliation of the Jews, they do not agree on the age and the mode of this occurrence. All we are told is that it shall happen. Why? St. Paul explains it. His prophecy is a message of consolation to everyone: "For the gifts and the call of God are without repentance" (Rom 11:29). Israel, once chosen, shall never escape.

According to Catholic teaching, therefore, the Jews, though rejecting the gospel and hence outside the community of salvation (they may be saved individually, like all other men, through an implicit desire for baptism) are, nevertheless, in some mysterious sense, still a people set apart for a blessing. The Church is the true Israel, it is she who is now God's holy people, the chosen people, the people of the covenant; but for all that the Bible announces that the Jews who refuse to believe do remain, in some sense, a consecrated community. The popular American translation of the New Testament, the Confraternity Edition, comments on St. Paul's phrase "The gifts and the call of God are without repentance" by adding: "The Jews remain the people of God's predilection, and will eventually be converted and saved."

When regarding the Jews with Christian eyes, therefore, we are bound to acknowledge the mysterious destiny which has been appointed for them, and to see in them the perpetual symbol of the mercy of God faithful to his promises. In the light of this scriptural hope the ancient legends of the rejection of the Jews and their everlasting punishment on this earth appear as grotesque deformations of the true doctrine. Since Christianity is the fulfillment, and hence replacement, of the ancient faith of Israel, since the Christian faith abrogates the Law and overthrows many of the institutions of Judaism, and since the controversy between the early Church and the Synagogue has left its mark on the shape of our Gospels, Christians are often exposed to the temptation of becoming anti-Jewish. It is for this reason that the doctrine of Israel's perpetual consecration is so important. It prevents Christians from ever despising the Jews. This is the reason why St. Paul revealed this mystery to the Gentile Christians of Rome: "lest you be wise in your own conceits" (Rom 11:25). The same concern is echoed by St. Thomas many centuries later when he asserts, "it would be harmful to the Christian people to be ignorant of this mystery." With this knowledge the struggle of Chritsians to replace Judaism can never deteriorate into an anti-Jewish movement; and if it does, it can do so only by being unfaithful to the gospel itself.

These three principles, drawn from the Scriptures and Catholic tradition, have emerged with full power in the sympathetic dialogue carried on between Christians and Jews. Christian writers have become aware of our own Jewish roots and of the loss of theological balance whenever we forget that the history of Israel is our own. Neglecting our Jewish origin, we tended to drift too far away from the Bible and biblical notions, and we were often unwilling to remember that God's ways with Israel in the Old Testament are still a pattern for his ways with the Church. While we live in the age of fulfillment present in Christ now, we are still awaiting the establishment of his kingdom in glory; and hence the passage of the children of Israel through the desert, their miraculous liberations, the wonderful gifts of food and drink, their revolts and their reconciliations—all have meaning for us still. These things are types of what God does, in a higher and more spiritual manner, in the Church, the new people of his choice. Whenever we forget this relationship, we tend to exaggerate the glory in which we live. We forget that the gifts of unity and holiness which the Church has received are never so full and final that the story of Israel's fall and restoration cannot, in some analogous sense, be applied to us. Not only do the Jews of old remind us of the lowliness and the relative un-fulfillment of our situation; even the Jews of our day recall to us the eschatological tension in which we live. The community of Christ is not yet complete without them, the end will not come yet. We must still wait. We are still under the judgment of God.

The movement within the Catholic Church (and within Protestant Churches) to correct the misunderstandings regarding the Jews and to announce again the consoling doctrine of the New Testament, has assumed such large proportions that it may well be called official. The recent popes have made several statements condemning anti-Semitism. According to the popes, the anti-Semite sins against Christian charity and sins in the order of faith, since he refuses to regard the Jewish people in the light of salvation history. The famous statement of Pius XI that "spiritually we are Semites" refers to the mystery that all believers in the Church are children of Abraham. In Christ we have entered the promises made to Israel. In Christ we truly belong to the family of God's first love. The Church is Israel. The

Pope's remark is just a modern paraphrase of the formula used in the liturgy of Holy Saturday expressing our joy that the *dignitas Israelitica* (the dignity of belonging to Israel) has been conferred upon all of us who believe. In a more practical way, the popes of our day endorsed the movement of rehabilitation when they made changes in liturgical formulas and gestures which had produced misunderstandings in the past. The best known among these changes is the suppression of the word *perfidia* and its derivatives from the prayers of the Good Friday liturgy. Even if *perfidia* originally meant simply unbelief, in modern languages it has come to stand for moral defect, for perfidy or treachery. It is also well known that the genuflection has been restored to the prayers for the Jews on Good Friday, since the omission, whatever its origin, was regarded by the people as a gesture of contempt. Pope John XXIII, receiving in audience a large group of American Jews, introduced himself by saying, "I am Joseph, your brother." On one level this is a play on words, since the Pope's Christian name is Joseph. But on a deeper level it is a confession that his and the Church's relationship to the Jews is theological, even if they are not aware of it. Without knowing it, the Jews are related to us. They are our brothers, in spite of their denial.

The movement of reforming the Christian approach to Israel has produced many visible effects on the diocesan level. I have already referred to the remarkable pastoral of Cardinal Lienart at Easter 1960, which was entirely dedicated to this subject. In countries such as Belgium, France, Germany, Holland, and Switzerland, the new catechisms and the approved books on religion for schools have undergone considerable modifications in their references to the Jewish people. These changes have been made in the light of a set of "ten points" which have received wide recognition. Shortly after the Second World War, an International Conference of Christians and Jews meeting at Seelisberg in Switzerland, still under the shock of the destruction of half the Jewish race, sought to formulate a set of principles guiding Christian teachers in their references to the Jews so that religious instruction would be more faithful to the gospel and prevent the Christian faith from being poisoned by a contempt for the Jewish people. The "ten points" are silent about the full Catholic belief about Jesus Christ; they are exclusively concerned with his human origins. If we keep in mind this limitation, the following "ten points" are suitable guides for Catholic teachers:

1. We must recall that one and the same God speaks to us in the Old and New Testament.

2. We must recall that Jesus (the eternal Son of God) was born of a Jewish mother, belonging to the family of David and the people of Israel, and that his everlasting love and mercy embrace his own people and the entire world.

3. We must recall that the first disciples, the apostles, and the earliest martyrs were Jews.

4. We must recall that the principal commandment of Christianity, the love of God and neighbor, which was announced in the Old Testament and confirmed (and elevated) by Jesus, is of equal obligation, in all human relations without exception, for Jews and Christians alike.

5. We must avoid belittling biblical and post-biblical Judaism as a means of exalting Christianity.

6. We must avoid using the word "Jews" in the exclusive meaning of "Jesus' enemies" and the words "the enemies of Jesus" to designate the Jewish people as a whole.

7. We must avoid presenting the passion of Jesus as if all Jews, or Jews only, have incurred the odium of the crucifixion. Not all Jews demanded the death of Jesus. Not only Jews were responsible for it. The cross, which saves humanity, reveals that Christ has died for the sins of all of us. Christian parents and teachers should be reminded of their great responsibility in telling the story of Jesus' suffering. By doing it in a superficial manner, they run

the risk of creating an aversion against others in the hearts of
their children or listeners. In a simple mind, moved by an ardent
love and compassion for the crucified Savior, a natural abhorrence
for Jesus' persecutors may easily turn, according to the laws of
psychology, into an indiscriminate hatred of the Jews of all times,
even of our own day.

8. We must avoid treating the condemnations of Scripture and the
   cry of the enraged crowds, "His blood be on us and our children," without recalling that this cry does not cancel the words
   of our Lord of incomparably greater consequence, "Father, forgive them, for they know not what they do."

9. We must avoid encouraging in any way the opinion that the
   Jews are a people accursed, reprobated, and set aside for perpetual suffering.

10. It must not be left unmentioned that the first members of the
    Church were Jews.

We see here that the dialogue between Christians and Jews
has produced tangible results in the Christian Church. The
question arises whether this dialogue has also initiated changes
in Judaism. Since there are so many trends and movements
within the Jewish people, varying from orthodox rabbinical
practice to the most radical modernism, and since, moreover, a
large section of the people do not believe in God, it is not at all
clear whether our question can be answered. It seems to me,
however, that among the great Jewish writers of our time, among
philosophers, theologians, and poets, among educated Jewish
families in most countries, the attitude toward Christianity and
Christ has undergone a remarkable transformation.

The literature on the changes in the Christian outlook on the
people of Israel is abundant. Much has been published by
Protestants and Catholics. There are special journals dedicated
exclusively to this field of study. There are, for example, the
Freiburger Rundbrief in Germany and the *Cahiers Sioniens* in

France. In the United States we have the Institute of Judaeo-Christian Studies directed by Msgr. John Oesterreicher. There is, however, comparatively little published on the changes within Judaism in regard to its outlook on Christianity.

The transformation is most obvious in European writers, both philosophical and artistic. Men like Martin Buber, Franz Rosenzweig, Hans Schoeps, Leo Beck, or, in the literary field, Franz Werfel, Franz Kafka, Stefan Zweig, Sholem Asch, have obviously been profoundly influenced by Christian literature. The dialogue with Christianity has enriched them: the new and positive attitude toward it is found in these men, even when they utterly repudiate the Christian faith and the idea of becoming Christian has never entered their mind. They are willing to listen, to learn, to discover the deep intentions of the gospel, the spiritual vision of the universe in the liturgy, and the cosmic and human transformation announced by Christ; and even when they reject these things, they find that much is relevant to their Jewish tradition.

A second area of change is the attitude of Jews to the person of Jesus. In the past Jewish writers and Jewish people in general observed an absolute silence about Jesus. They would not mention his name or study his gospel. Christian persecution and slander had hurt them so much that the name of Christ inspired them with horror and fear. In modern Jewish writers the change is remarkable. The best study on this subject, easily available in English, is a section of the important book *The Jewish People and Jesus Christ* by the learned Dr. Jakob Jocz of Toronto. The whole field, however, has not been treated exhaustively. It is to be hoped that such an investigation will be undertaken one day by a scholar of Jewish faith. It is remarkable that wherever we turn in Jewish literature, we find the appreciation of Jesus as a great Jew, as a man who elected the most spiritual elements of Judaism and whose ethical doctrine can only be understood against the background of the Jewish currents of his day. Recent scholarship has brought to light that Jewish spirituality at the time of Jesus was more varied, alive, and fruitful than might appear from the prophetical threats of the New Testament, and Jews have become conscious that Jesus fits into this background. They find parallels for his sayings and attitudes in other rabbis. We believe that this appraisal does not really come to grips with the mystery of the man Jesus; a purely literary approach is insensitive to the core of Christ's personality. But the open and positive outlook on the Son of Man is something new in Jewish literature.

There is a third effect of Jewish-Christian dialogue. While we cannot emphasize enough that this dialogue is not carried on with the intention of converting Jews to Christianity, we do not deny that the Catholic Church has exerted a tremendous fascination on the Jews of western Europe in the last few decades. Many of the great philosophers and writers among the Jews have come close to her, though only a few have actually accepted baptism. John Oesterreicher's well-known book *The Walls Are Crumbling* tells us the story of seven great Jewish philosophers, all of whom have felt the attraction of the Church, first of her liturgical and spiritual tradition, and then of the person of Jesus who is the divine ground for this tradition. Names such as Henri Bergson, Edmund Husserl, Simone Weil, and Edith Stein have become famous in the history of contemporary culture. This is not the purpose of the dialogue, but it is inevitable that those who study the gospel of Christ will discover a deep and abiding sympathy for it.

The enrichment of Judaism through Christian thought, the new appreciation of the person of Jesus, and the attraction exerted by many elements of Christianity are three observable changes which the dialogue has produced among the Jews. These attitudes begin to reach to the level of schools and synagogues. I wish to quote from the spiritually significant book by Emil Fackenheim called *Paths to Jewish Belief*, a little work written for young people to be instructed in the Jewish religion. This beautiful book is inconceivable without a preceding inner dialogue with Christianity. Fackenheim, of course, rejects the Christian creed. He writes: "The Jew finds in Judaism the supreme expression of ethics and morality, of love of God and concern for his fellow man. At the same time, Judaism shares much with Christianity, and the Jew cannot but have regard for this religion." The style of the book reflects a deep reverence for the great Christian literature of faith, and many themes explored by Christian writers are used to portray more faithfully the mystery of Jewish religion. The author is so deeply sympathetic toward Christianity that he can use these generous words: "Jews have often been persecuted in Christian countries. This fact has made many Jews adopt a very negative attitude toward Christianity as a whole. The truth is, of course, that Christianity is deeply opposed to persecution in any form, and that anyone who persecutes cannot call himself a true Christian." The author denies that Jesus is the Jewish messias. But explaining to the young people of the synagogue the difference between Judaism and Christianity, he speaks of the claims of Jesus. He writers, "Jesus himself was convinced that he was the long-awaited deliverer. His message, too, was impressive. It addressed itself, above all, to those to whom the messianic message would be most meaningful—the poor, the sick, the downtrodden. . . . And it was delivered with the kind of strength which flows only from unfaltering faith."

Though there can be no real *rapprochement* between Judaism and Christianity—they are deeply divided by their attitude toward Christ—dialogue is obviously not in vain.

APPENDIX I

Pastoral Letter on the Responsibilities of Catholics with Regard to Christian Unity

by Paul-Emile Cardinal Leger,
Archbishop of Montreal

Dear Brethren:

The day before he died, after having instituted the Eucharist, sacrament of unity, Jesus Our Saviour offered up to his Father this prayer which was also the testament of the love which he had for his own: "That they all may be one, as thou, Father, in me, and I in thee; that they all may be one in us; that the world may believe that thou hast sent me" (1). This last will of the Master has always been considered an obligation for his Church. At the very beginning of the Christian era, the brethren of the first Christian community, Jerusalem, "had but one heart and one soul" (2). The apostle Paul urged the communities which he founded, to be "eager to preserve that unity the Spirit gives you, whose bond is peace" and to avoid all discord and coterie because "you are one body with a single spirit; each of you . . . called in the same hope; with the same Lord, the same faith, the same baptism, with the same God, the same Father of all of us, who is above all beings, pervades all things, and lives in all of us" (3).

(1) John XVII, 21.   (2) Acts IV, 32.   (3) Ephesians IV, 3-6.

Unfortunately, from the very beginning, the sin of men introduced into the first communities ferments of disunity. The sad history of the separation of Christians is well known, especially the history of the schism between the East and the West in the eleventh century, and that which shattered the unity of Western Christianity in the sixteenth century as well as the innumerable divisions which followed in the various Protestant Churches.

The Church of Christ has never resigned itself to this state of things. She, and all Christians who set their heart upon following the will of the Lord, have constantly sought to heal the wounds caused by disunion.

I believe it would not be an exaggeration to say that concern for unity has become the major quality of contemporary Christianity. All are aware of the extraordinary extension of the ecumenical movement. In this respect, and just recently, two events of great importance took place: the Pan-Orthodox Conference of Rhodes in September 1961, which gathered together the Bishops of all the Orthodox Churches of the Eastern Rites; and a short time later, in November of last year, the general meeting of the World Council of Churches at New Delhi which brought together delegates of the great majority of non-Catholic Churches and, for the first time, five official Catholic observers. You will recall that, on November 14th last, we had recommended to your prayers this general assembly of the World Council of Churches.

A third event—this one concerns us more directly—has been in preparation for several years: the Second Vatican Council. This Council has as its principal objective the internal renewal of the Church and, consequently, it aims to facilitate the reconciliation and reunion of Christians. The Council, according to John XXIII "will surely be a wonderful manifestation of truth, unity and charity: a manifestation indeed which we hope will be received by those who are separated from the Apostolic See as a gentle invitation to seek and find that unity for which Jesus Christ prayed so ardently to the Heavenly Father" (4).

It is with great pleasure that We behold, in Our diocese, a strengthening of the ecumenical spirit. For the last several years, thanks to the apostolic zeal of the St. Paul Committee, the Church Unity Octave of prayer for unity has been more widely observed. There is more sympathy between the leaders of the various Christian religions and it is with pleasure that we behold Catholic priests and Protestant clergymen gathering together more frequently for fraternal dialogue. The press and modern communications media, radio and television, have shown a great interest in the problems of Church unity and have given them wide diffusion.

Conscious of the importance of this movement, We feel it a duty of Our pastoral charge to give it the leadership which it needs. We invite you to reflect with Us upon this mystery of Church unity and the division of Christians and We urge you to seek out with Us the ways which will help us all to continue, according to our abilities, in this great work of God.

I. THE UNITY AND DISUNITY OF CHRISTIANS

When we consider the population of the world, we are astonished to see, after nearly twenty centuries of Christianity, that barely one third of humanity is Christian. In a world population of about three billion, there are only about one billion who are Christians. At first sight, this latter group might seem large, but we find that, besides being limited nearly entirely to the Western world, it is divided in three: Catholics (about 510,000,-000), Orthodox (about 200,000,000) and Protestants (about 240,000,000). There are further divisions among the Christians

(4) Encyclical *Ad Petri Cathedram*, June 29, 1959.

of this latter group such as: Anglicans, Lutherans, Calvinists, without mentioning the many other Protestant groups which are less numerous.

The external disunity of the Christian world is itself the manifestation of more profound differences of belief concerning the hierarchical government of the Church, divine worship and some essential points of doctrine. Though we believe firmly that the Roman Catholic Church is the only one which is "apostolic," this is not the conviction of members of the Protestant or Orthodox faiths. Though the Orthodox share our belief in the episcopal structure of the Church of Christ, they refuse to grant to the Bishop of Rome the rights which are recognized as his in Catholic doctrine. As for the great majority of Protestants, they do not agree with us or with the Orthodox concerning the very structure of the Church of Christ. And yet all claim to be followers of Christ and are proud to be called Christians.

By baptism validly received, men are inserted into Christ and become one body with him: "we too, all of us, have been baptized into a single body by the power of a single spirit" (5). Moreover, the Council of Florence echoed this doctrine of Saint Paul when it declared that baptism "is the gateway to the spiritual life; by it, in fact, we become members of Christ and belong to the Body of the Church" (6).

Grafted onto Christ, become one body with him, Christians are members one of the other. But their unity must also be effected in the same belief, in the reception of the same sacraments and in the charity which unites all baptized Christians under the guidance of the same shepherds, united among themselves, and with the one who continues the mission of Peter who was the unifying element in the apostolic college.

And it is here that division occurs. If it is true that every serious sin introduces between the sinner and the Body of Christ

(5) I Corinthians XII, 13.
(6) Council of Florence, *Decree to the Armenians,* Denzinger 696.

a ferment of disunity, there are some sins that go directly against unity: sins against the faith and against Church union. Thus, the one who voluntarily breaks from the faith and from Church union places himself, with reference to Christ and his Church, in a state of violent separation. Even the one who is separated from the true Church through no fault of his own, finds himself involuntarily deprived of full communion with Christ. Herein lies the paradox and the tragedy of the situation: a tear in the seamless robe of Christ!

On the one hand all Christians, by virtue of their baptism, are attached to Christ and his Church for the baptismal character is indelible; on the other hand, because of divergence of belief and the breaking off of communion within the Church, they are deprived of the plentitude of the benefits which can be reaped only in complete unity. Deprived of unity, how can they avoid dispersion and error?

II. THE EVIL OF DISUNITY

Faced with such a situation, the Church cannot remain indifferent. Conscious of the expressed will of Christ, aware of the scandal which the disunity of Christians gives to the non-Christian world and the evil which it brings to those who are separated from it and those who have remained within it, the Church feels the urgent need to do everything within its power to help heal this wound. For disunity is an evil.

It is an evil first of all for the separated brethren who are no longer in full possession of the ordinary means of salvation. Even those who remain within the unity of the true Church cannot but suffer the consequences of the separation of their brethren. Doubtless the body of Christ is not substantially affected by the division of Christians, but it remains nonetheless true that the Church, in its concrete life, is limited in the exercise of its role as witness of Christ. It is deprived of all that could be brought to it by that multitude of separated brethren who are sincerely desirous of serving God in spirit and in truth, according to their own manner of thinking, feeling and praying.

In the midst of the polemics which spring from disunity, the Church's theological thinking itself is often exposed to the danger of concentrating too exclusively on points which are questioned thus stiffening its positions. In such a combination of circumstances, it will often take centuries to see the consequences of our disunity, achieve a more balanced doctrinal presentation and rediscover the values which have been left in the background.

But for us the most serious consequence of division is doubtless that the Catholic Church our Mother is, in the eyes of non-Christians, but one of the numerous Christian denominations, even though it be the most important numerically. It is because Christians present to the world the sad spectacle of their division, that the pagan world has not believed in Him whom the Father has sent, his Son Jesus Christ (7).

III. THE ATTITUDE OF GOD'S PEOPLE
WITH REGARD TO DISUNITY

The Church is constantly preoccupied and anxious about the reunion of divided Christianity. Though this responsibility lies especially upon the Successor of Peter and all the Bishops, it is nonetheless true that all the members of the Church are called to play an important and essential role in the search for full unity among Christians. But how are they to fulfill this role?

Internal Renewal.

The first thing to be done concerns the life of the Church and each of its members. According to the view of Pope John XXIII,

(7) Cf. John XVII, 21.

a return to unity of separated Christians is linked to the internal renewal of the Catholic Church—a renewal which he has described in his Encyclical *Ad Petri Cathedram* as "a development of Catholic faith, a moral renewal of the Christian life of the faithful, an adaptation of ecclesiastical discipline to the needs and methods of our time" (8). This, according to the Holy Father, is the way to restore to the face of the Church all its splendor and to open to our separated brethren the avenues of reconciliation and return (9).

What each one of us must do is draw upon the Gospel and make it the inspiration of our whole life. Our life must truly be the mirror of the charity of Christ; it must be filled with love for God and men, our brothers, on the individual and family level as well as on a social and international level. Our Christian life must be nourished by the purest fountains—the Word of God and the liturgy. Let us make our lives honest, loyal, virtuous and devoted. Let our lives be centered upon the essential realities of our faith and not upon peripheral devotions. In a word, let us ask God to transform us, as individuals and members of the Church, into Christ Jesus, the bright image of the Father.

If this renewal is to be effected in reality, it is necessary that it be based upon harmoniously balanced doctrine and rooted in the Word of God, the tradition of the Fathers and the life of God's people, as interpreted by the Church which is the guardian of truth. Thus, our faith should be essentially centered upon the mystery of salvation, that mystery which was hidden from past centuries and fulfilled in Christ Jesus (10).

Our faith, it is true, demands adhesion to a certain number of dogmas, but we must not forget that Christian faith is above all a way of life, a living contact with the Lord. In fact, do not the dogmas themselves express vital realities?

(8) *Ad Petri Cathedram*, June 29, 1959.
(9) Address to the Catholic Action Presidents of Italy, 1959.
(10) Cf. Romans XVI, 25–26.

This is the doctrine that must be presented by those who have been called by the Bishops to share in their apostolic mission. And all the faithful must align their faith with these perspectives.

Let us not allow our faith to dwell exclusively upon aspects of belief which appeal to religious emotivity, but rather seek above all to attain its central objective: the manifestation of the love of God for sinners in the death and resurrection of his Son. Placed in such perspective, even the dogmas which our separated brethren do not share with us, such as those concerning the privileges of Mary or the successor of Peter, might cease to be an obstacle to the reconciliation of separated Christians.

Charity and ecumenical dialogue.

If the wish to share in effecting the reunion of the members of Christ's Body places upon the Catholic an obligation to renew his life and to reach a better understanding of doctrine, it also requires that he come into contact with his separated brethren. No Christian who is animated by the charity of Christ can look upon his separated brethren as strangers or enemies. He must avoid all that can hurt them and widen the trench which separates us. He must rid himself of historical and psychological prejudices. He must seek in every way to love his separated brethren as brothers in Christ.

On the other hand, Catholic theologians must, under the vigilance of their bishops, seek to establish a dialogue with theologians of other Christian religions. The purpose of this dialogue is not to win arguments or to convert. Those who undertake such conversations seek, in mutual understanding, to discover the positive insights in the belief of their brethren. Evidently, there can be no question of promoting indifferentism or false irenics but rather of understanding from the inside, by being as objective as possible, the position of the other in order to comply with his legitimate claims. If we have such a reverent attitude, we shall then be in a position to expect the same dispositions of our brethren and be able to present to them our own position with the assurance that it will be received in the same spirit. Veritable dialogue consists in listening, and being listened to, with a will to narrow the gap and, if possible, to reach an identity of views.

Prayer for unity.

Concern about unity brings to mind the necessity of the renewal of Christian life and of ecumenical dialogue. We must not forget, however, that the unity of Christians will be brought about not by human effort but by the power of God. We know that all we ask the Father in the name of Our Lord Jesus Christ will certainly be granted to us if it be in conformity with the eternal plan of God. Now, is there in the Gospel a clearer expression of the will of God than his desire for the unity of all the disciples of Christ? It is Jesus himself who tells us of this desire in his prayer to the Father at the beginning of his Sacred Passion (11). To obtain from the Father the grace of unity, prayer is therefore the principal means and the most efficacious.

But if this prayer is to be answered, it must have certain qualities. It must be a prolongation of the very prayer of Christ, associate itself completely with it and come, as it were, from the very depths of the Heart of Jesus. All our human ambitions must be cast aside and our prayer blend with the intentions of the Lord whose ultimate objective is the unity of all Christians in one Church in some mysterious way which we do not yet understand.

Our prayer, filled with joyous hope—because we know with certitude that the Father will grant it one day—must also be humble and patient. On the human level, unity seems to be extremely difficult and remote. All impatience can only foster undue precipitation which leads to bitter disillusion.

Finally, besides being rooted in a great love of Christ and of our separated brethren, our prayer must be animated by re-

(11) Cf. John XVII, 21.

pentance and sorrow, for we are all responsible for the disunity of Christians. As suggested by His Holiness, Pope John XXIII, it is not for us to make an historical investigation into these divisions, nor to try to find out "who was wrong" or "who was right." We all share in the responsibility(12).

The Church Unity Octave.

Though we join with the Church in Christ's prayer for unity every day at the canon of the Mass, there is a period of the year when we have the occasion to pray for that intention with particular intensity and in union with all who invoke the name of Our Lord and Saviour Jesus Christ. This period is known as the Church Unity Octave which is observed from January 18th to January 25th.

Thus, during these days, the prayers of the whole world will converge on the way to the Father, asking him to bring about, according to his Will and by whatever means he wants, his eternal plan of unity. This year, moreover, we have a very special reason to join in this concerted universal supplication, for we are at the threshold of a Council one of whose principal objectives is to foster Christian reunion. To encourage the faithful and the clergy of Our diocese in their zeal for this cause, We have deemed it opportune to command that the votive Mass *Pro unitate ecclesiae* be celebrated as the principal Mass on Sunday, January 21, and that the prayer of this same votive Mass be recited as the *Oratio imperata* from January 18th to January 25th.

Besides joining in these liturgical prayers, all the faithful of the diocese should make every effort to pray individually and collectively for unity. Let there be organized in the churches, oratories and chapels, in the institutions of the diocese, a veritable campaign of prayer for unity. Let us often repeat with great fervour, during the octave, the prayer which the priest addresses

(12) Address of His Holiness Pope John XXIII to the Pastors of Rome, January 29, 1959.

to Jesus, the fountain of unity, a few moments before receiving his Body in Holy Communion: "Lord Jesus Christ, who have said to your Apostles: My peace I give you, my peace I leave unto you; do not look upon my sins, but on the faith of Thy Church, and graciously give Her peace and unity in accordance with Thy will."

APPENDIX II*

Pastoral Letter on Racial Prejudice

by Achille Cardinal Liénart,
Bishop of Lille

My Brethren:

Recently, acts of hostility were perpetrated against the Jews in various countries: in Germany, in England, in Belgium, in Italy, and in France, too. Swastikas, Jewish stars, and anti-Jewish slogans were put on the walls of synagogues; one synagogue was even set on fire. We cannot but deplore these acts, particularly because they are the disquieting signs of a returning anti-Semitism, the height of whose outrages we witnessed during the last war. In those days, Jewish families were deported en masse under frightful conditions, and several millions of men, women, and children were put to death in the gas chambers of Germany—men, women, and children whom their tormentors could charge with no other crime than that they were of Jewish stock.

Christians must be clear of complicity with so dangerous a state of mind, despite the religious pretexts behind which it occasionally takes cover. Now that this frame of mind has made its reappearance, it seems timely that we warn you against it and, with the help of this letter, explain to you the little known

* From John M. Oesterreicher, ed., *The Bridge: A Yearbook of Judaeo-Christian Studies,* Vol. IV (New York: Pantheon Books, 1962), pp. 347–52.

doctrine of the Church on the destiny of the Jewish people. This doctrine obliges us to reject anti-Semitism absolutely, from the human as well as the religious point of view, and to adopt toward the Jewish people an attitude that is the very opposite of anti-Semitism, the attitude of respect and love.

Looking at it from the human point of view, anti-Semitism exploits the evil instinct that so easily sets the various families of mankind against each other. There are those for which we feel a natural attraction and there are others which arouse in us antipathy or contempt.

Such antipathy is evident in the way we look at the black or the yellow peoples, at the North Africans or even at some of the European nations beside us. More often still, such antipathy brands our relationship toward the Jewish people who, dispersed among all the nations, yet preserve in our midst their ethnic characteristics, their own mentality, their customs, their religion.

Let us be on guard against this blind racism, the source of so much injustice and enmity. When we experience it within ourselves, as everyone does, we must rid ourselves of it; we must do so, chiefly because of our Christian faith. We know that all men, despite the diversity of races, are members of the same humankind created by God in unity; that all men are our brothers; that they all have a right to our respect and our love. Moreover, we believe in a universal redemption: In and through it, Christ Jesus, our Saviour and Head, calls all men without distinction to form but one single people of God. Within its ranks there is, according to St. Paul, no longer Jew or Greek, man or woman, slave or freeman (see Gal 3:28), but one single humanity wholly joined in Christ and summoned to realize its common, supernatural destiny.

In such a perspective, there is no room for anti-Semitism; the religious pretexts some try to invoke cannot alter this truth.

Hence we must defend ourselves against the ready-made, far too simple idea that the Jewish people have become a people cursed by God because, through their responsible leaders, they rejected the promised Messiah in the person of Jesus; worse still, that they are a nation of deicides because they made the Son of God die upon the cross. From premises like these the conclusion may easily be drawn that they deserve the contempt and hostility of Christ's faithful disciples. And from there, it is only a short step to the assumption that anything is permitted to make them pay for their crime.

The true doctrine of the Church is entirely different; the attitude she demands toward the Jewish people is exactly the opposite of this spirit of reprisal.

It is not true that the Jewish people bears the first and only responsibility for the death of Jesus. The deepest cause of His death upon the cross is the sins of men. Consequently, we are all responsible; the Jews were only our delegates.

Nor is it true that the Jews are deicides, for had they been aware of His divinity they would have believed in Him and would not have made Him die.

This unawareness earned for them Jesus' own forebearance: "Father, forgive them, for they do not know what they are doing" (Lk 23:34). His apostles, too, proclaimed this unawareness in the presence of the people of Jerusalem, immediately after Pentecost. "You disowned the Holy and Just One," St. Peter told them in one of his first sermons. "The author of life you killed. . . . And now, brethren, I know that you acted in ignorance, as did also your rulers. But in this way God fulfilled what He had announced beforehand by the mouth of all the prophets, namely, that His Christ should suffer. Repent therefore and be converted, that your sins may be blotted out" (Ac 3:14–19).

It would be even more unjust to hold the entire Jewish people responsible, those of today as those of Jesus' day, and to forget our debt to them. Through them the whole revelation of God's plan in the Old Testament came to us, and through them we inherited the divine promises. Their prophets are our prophets. Their psalms have become our prayer. They are the stock to which our divine Founder belongs as man: Jesus, Son of David, our Saviour. And so does the Blessed Virgin Mary, our Mother; so do St. Joseph, the Twelve, St. Paul, and the infant Church of Jerusalem. "Spiritually, we are Semites," said Pope Pius XI. Lest we deny our origin and commit an injustice, we must not turn the Jewish people over to a collective reprobation.

Nor is it true that Israel, the chosen people of the Old Covenant, has become an accursed people in the New.

Actually, the religious destiny of Israel is a mystery of grace, and we Christians ought to ponder it with respectful sympathy.

No one experienced this drama more painfully than did St. Paul, the former Pharisee, the Jew who could say of himself that he had shown much more zeal for the traditions of his fathers than had many of his contemporaries (see Gal 1:14). By God's grace converted on the road to Damascus, he felt in his innermost being the misfortune of his brethren dwelling in incredulity. With all his soul, he sought to understand God's mysterious designs for His chosen people. In chapters 9 to 11 of the Epistle to the Romans, he discloses the secret of His designs to us, and his teaching is so full of hope for the Jewish people, so full of instruction for us, that we can do no better than receive and follow it.

But what was Israel's fault, according to St. Paul? To have thought that she could save herself by observing the commandments of the Law, although salvation is God's free gift, a gift obtained by faith in His promises and in the Christ who made them reality. She was wrong not to believe and, since then, has left her road and is astray.

Does it follow, then, that Israel has been irrevocably rejected by God? Far from it, says St. Paul, for God is faithful and His gifts are without repentance (see Rom 11:29). He never takes them back. Israel has not become a people accursed but remains the chosen people. The thread of her destiny has not been severed; it is only suspended.

Has the straying of His people hindered the unfolding of God's work? Quite the opposite. It has given the redemptive work greater breadth. For a new phase has begun: the entrance of the pagan peoples into the Church of Jesus Christ. Now all the nations are admitted to membership in the new people of God and are summoned to extend it to the ends of the world and to the end of time. They have been grafted, as it were, upon the old trunk of Israel, deprived of its natural branches, in order to draw life from its sap and make it bloom even more richly. But when the full number of Gentiles have been grafted into the trunk (see Rom 11:25), the day will have come for Israel to be placed again by God on the tree of salvation and to resume the course of her providential destiny.

"Oh, the depth of the riches of the wisdom and of the knowledge of God!" St. Paul cries out before the splendor of this divine plan. "How incomprehensible are His judgments and how unsearchable His ways! . . . To Him be the glory forever" (Rom 11:33–36).

Since we are Christians because of Israel's momentary effacement, we must recoil from self-glorification at her expense. We must not set ourselves up against her, rather ought we remember that if God permitted the natural branches to fall so tragically, He could cut us off, too, should we be unfaithful. To understand this mystery is to be inspired to personal humility and to love for Israel.

Some may find, my dear brethren, that in today's world, beset by grave internal and external conflicts, the problem of anti-Semitism does not warrant that we engage your attention upon it. You, at least, will understand that the Church cannot suppress what she reads in holy Scripture. Besides, I believe that the conclusion to be drawn from the Church's teaching on this particular point is of sufficiently universal bearing. It tells us what attitude we, as Christians, ought to adopt toward the most serious problems of the present world and what immense service we may render, provided we remain faithful to the Gospel.

In a Christian soul the spirit of racism has no place. Not only must we not hate or disdain the Jews, the North Africans, the Negroes or any people of this earth—we must love them as brothers and respect their human dignity. For we are all created in the image of God, we are all called in Jesus Christ to the same destiny of sonship in God.

Nor can there be class hatred in the soul of a Christian for, as St. Paul says, there is now no longer slave, no longer freeman, but a single people of God. When legitimate interests between men or nations clash, a Christian is not permitted to resolve such differences simply by "the right of the stronger." He must resolve differences in the spirit of mutual justice and love, as is the way of brothers who respect one another. Above all things, we must never injure the dignity of persons, be it physically by violence to their bodies or properties, be it morally by treating them like inferior beings or subjecting them to offensive humiliations.

We must even be prepared to forgive our enemies.

It is not in the ranks of "antis," whatever their banners, that the Christian ought to combat, for though the Church fights error she does not fight men. On the contrary, she invites us to place ourselves at the service of universal love, which our Lord Jesus Christ made His supreme command. His disciples are obliged to love all men and all nations; they also have the mission of spreading throughout the world the meaning of the equality of all men before God.

Who cannot see how urgent this task is and how much it deserves our dedication? The world we live in is unhappy. The divisions and hatreds that rend it apart only multiply its sufferings, and this because men no longer know how to love one another. Let us, then, take the Lord's commandment seriously. Let us be of those who truly love one another. Thus we shall draw men along the only road leading to that peace everyone longs for: the peace of Christ.

Lent, 1960

BIBLIOGRAPHY

Adam, Karl, *One and Holy*, trans. by Cecily Hastings. New York, Sheed and Ward, 1951.

Baum, Gregory, *That They May Be One*. Westminster, Md., Newman Press, 1958.

Baum, Gregory, *The Jews and the Gospel*. Westminster, Md., Newman Press, 1961.

Bouyer, Louis, *The Spirit and Forms of Protestantism*, trans. by A. V. Littledale. Westminster, Md., Newman Press, 1956.

Bouyer, Louis, *The Word, Church and Sacraments in Protestantism and Catholicism*, trans. by A. V. Littledale. New York, Desclee, 1961.

* Brown, Robert McAfee, *The Spirit of Protestantism*. New York, Oxford University Press, 1961.

Callahan, Daniel, and others, eds., *Christianity Divided*. New York, Sheed and Ward, 1961.

Congar, Yves, *The Mystery of the Church*, trans. by A. V. Littledale. Baltimore, Helicon Press, 1960.

Congar, Yves, *The Wide World, My Parish*, trans. by Donald Attwater. Baltimore, Helicon Press, 1961.

* Dillenberger, John, and Welch, Claude, *Protestant Christianity*. New York, Charles Scribner's Sons, 1958.

Dumont, C. J., *Approaches to Christian Unity,* trans. by Henry St. John. Baltimore, Helicon Press, 1959.

* Goodall, Norman, *The Ecumenical Movement.* New York, Oxford University Press, 1961.

Hardon, John, *Christianity in Conflict.* Westminster, Md., Newman Press, 1959.

Knox, Ronald, *Enthusiasm.* New York, Oxford University Press, 1950.

Leeming, Bernard, *The Churches and the Church.* Westminster, Md., Newman Press, 1960.

* Minear, Paul, ed., *The Nature of the Unity We Seek.* St. Louis, Bethany Press, 1958.

* Molland, Einar, *Christendom.* New York, Philosophical Library, 1959.

* Nelson, John Robert, ed., *Christian Unity in North America.* St. Louis, Bethany Press, 1958.

Pol, Willem van de, *The Christian Dilemma,* trans. by G. van Hall. New York, Philosophical Library, 1952.

St. John, Henry, *Essays in Christian Unity.* Westminster, Md., Newman Press, 1955.

* Skydsgaard, K. E., *One in Christ,* trans. by Axel C. Kildegard. Philadelphia, Muhlenberg Press, 1957.

Tavard, George, *The Catholic Approach to Protestantism.* New York, Harper & Brothers, 1955.

Tavard, George, *Protestantism,* trans. by Rachel Attwater. New York, Hawthorn Books, 1959.

Tavard, George, *Holy Writ or Holy Church.* New York, Harper & Brothers, 1960.

Tavard, George, *Two Centuries of Ecumenism,* trans. by Royce W. Hughes. Notre Dame, Ind., Fides Publishers Assn., 1960.

* Torrance, Thomas, *Conflict and Agreement in the Church,* 2 vols. Naperville, Ill., Alec R. Allenson, Inc., 1959–60.

Weigel, Gustave, *A Survey of Protestant Theology in Our Day.* Westminster, Md., Newman Press, 1954.

Weigel, Gustave, *Faith and Understanding in America.* New York, Macmillan Co., 1959.

Weigel, Gustave, *Catholic Theology in Dialogue.* New York, Harper & Brothers, 1961.

Weigel, Gustave, and Brown, Robert McAfee, *An American Dialogue.* Garden City, N. Y., Doubleday & Co., Inc., 1960.

* Protestant authors.